DOCE ME STATUTA TUA

BRADFIELD COLLEGE LIBRARY

W. B. Yeats
Metaphysician as Dramatist

Heather C. Martin

W. B. Yeats spent a great deal of his life immersing himself in magical, mystical, and philosophic studies in order, as he claimed, to devise a personal system of thought "that would leave [his] . . . imagination free to create as it chose and yet make all that it created, or could create, part of the one history, and that the soul's." He succeeded in developing a cohesive metaphysics, and one which is surprisingly original. While he set it down in a series of philosophical treatises culminating in *A Vision*, it is most clearly elaborated in his plays, which breathe life and meaning into the rather obscure statements of the treatises.

In this book, the author traces "the history of the soul" as it is developed in Yeats's plays. She elucidates the underlying system of thought in the drama and establishes its importance to the aim and execution of the plays by drawing attention to a few of the central themes, metaphors, and symbols through which it is developed.

The manuscript and the earliest published versions of the plays are indispensable to this study as they retain much of the abstract thought which Yeats eliminated from the later versions. Martin traces the development of the metaphors and images which gradually replaced Yeats's abstractions. In the process, she is able to uncover new meaning in the plays, as many subtle and obscure passages become clearly understandable.

Heather C. Martin is a writer living on Galiano Island, British Columbia, and a former Post-Doctoral Fellow with the Social Sciences and Humanities Research Council.

W.B. YEATS

Metaphysician as Dramatist

Heather C. Martin

COLIN SMYTHE
Gerrards Cross, 1986

First published in Great Britain in 1986 by
Colin Smythe Limited, Gerrards Cross, Buckinghamshire

British Library Cataloguing in Publication Data

Martin, Heather Carmen
    W. B. Yeats : metaphysician as dramatist.
    1. Yeats, W. B. — Dramatic works
    I. Title
    822'.8   PR5908.D7

    ISBN 0-86140-262-6

Copyright © 1986

WILFRID LAURIER UNIVERSITY PRESS
Waterloo, Ontario, Canada   N2L 3C5

86 87 88 89 4 3 2 1

Cover design by David Antscherl

Printed in Canada

Acknowledgments to copyright holders appear on pp. vii and viii.

Contents

Acknowledgments

I want to thank Donald Donaldson of the University of New Brunswick for introducing me to Yeats's drama fifteen years ago, Andrew Parkin of the University of British Columbia for his unflagging and cheerful guidance and encouragement, and George Mills Harper for first suggesting that I seek publication for my work on Yeats.

I am grateful to the Social Sciences and Humanities Research Council of Canada for a Post-Doctoral Fellowship which allowed me to further my work on Yeats. This book has been published with the help of a grant from the Canadian Federation for the Humanities, using funds provided by the Social Sciences and Humanities Research Council of Canada.

Most of all, I want to express my gratitude to my sparring partner, Bill Nemtin, without whose support and inspiration this book would have remained a set of boxes gathering dust in a corner.

Part of Chapter 4 originally appeared as "Of Flood and Fire: A Study of W. B. Yeats's *The Player Queen*," *The Canadian Journal of Irish Studies* 7, no. 1 (1981), and part of Chapter 2 as "W. B. Yeats: More Realist than Idealist," *The Canadian Journal of Irish Studies* 9, no. 2 (1983).

For permission to reprint copyrighted material the following acknowledgments are gratefully made:

- excerpts from "Chosen," "Phases of the Moon," and "All Souls' Night" are reprinted with permission of Macmillan Publishing Company from *Collected Poems* by W. B. Yeats; copyright 1918, 1919, 1924, 1928, 1933 by Macmillan Publishing Company, renewed 1946, 1947, 1952, 1956, 1961 by Bertha Georgie Yeats; copyright 1940 by Georgie Yeats, renewed 1968 by Bertha Georgie Yeats, Michael Butler Yeats, and Anne Yeats;

- excerpts from *Collected Plays* by W. B. Yeats are reprinted with permission of Macmillan Publishing Company; copyright 1934, 1952 by Macmillan Publishing Company; copyrights renewed 1962 by Bertha Georgie Yeats, and 1980 by Anne Yeats;

Abbreviations

A	Yeats, William Butler. *Autobiographies*. London: Macmillan, 1955.
AV (A)	———— . *A Vision*. London: T. Werner Laurie, 1925.
AV (B)	———— . *A Vision*. London: Macmillan, 1937.
Candle	Russell, George (AE). *The Candle of Vision*. Wheaton, Ill.: Theosophical Publishing House, 1965 (1st ed., 1918).
CMK	Kalogera, L. "Yeats's Celtic Mysteries." Ph.D. dissertation, Florida State University, 1977. (An edition of the notes and rituals for Yeats's Celtic Magical Order.)
CP	Yeats, William Butler. *Collected Poems of W. B. Yeats*. 2d ed. London: Macmillan, 1950.
DrC	Sidnell, Michael J., George P. Mayhew, and David R. Clark. *Druid Craft: The Writing of "The Shadowy Waters." Manuscripts of W. B. Yeats I*. Edited by David R. Clark. Dublin: Dolmen Press, 1971.
DWL	Yeats, William Butler. *Letters on Poetry from W. B. Yeats to Dorothy Wellesley*. London: Oxford University Press, 1940.
EI	———— . *Essays and Introductions*. London: Macmillan, 1961.
FFT	———— , ed. *Fairy and Folk Tales of the Irish Peasantry*. New York: Macmillan, 1973.
L	Wade, Allan, ed. *The Letters of W. B. Yeats*. New York: Macmillan, 1955.
M	Yeats, William Butler. *Mythologies*. London: Macmillan, 1959.
Memoirs	Donoghue, Denis, transcriber and ed. *Memoirs of W. B. Yeats*. New York: Macmillan, 1973.
MPQ	Bradford, Curtis B., transcriber and ed. *W. B. Yeats: The Writing of the Player Queen*. Dekalb: Northern Illinois University Press, 1977.
MRL	McHugh, Roger, ed. *Ah Sweet Dancer: W. B. Yeats, Margot Ruddock – A Correspondence*. New York: Macmillan, 1970.
SB	O'Donnell, William H., ed. *The Speckled Bird with Variant Versions*. Toronto: McClelland & Stewart, 1976.

TPBS   Clark, David R., and George P. Mayhew, eds. *A Tower of Polished Black Stones: Early Version of "The Shadowy Waters."* Dublin: Dolmen Press, 1971.

TSML   Bridges, Ursula, ed. *W. B. Yeats and T. Sturge Moore, Their Correspondence 1901-1937.* New York: Oxford University Press, 1953.

UP I   Frayne, John P., ed. *Uncollected Prose of W. B. Yeats.* Vol. 1. New York: Columbia University Press, 1970.

UP II   Frayne, John P., and Colton Johnson, eds. *Uncollected Prose of W. B. Yeats.* Vol. 2. London: Macmillan, 1975.

VB I and II   Gregory, Lady Isabella Augusta. *Visions and Beliefs in the West of Ireland.* With two essays and notes by W. B. Yeats. 2 vols. London: Putnam, 1920.

VE   Allt, P., and R. K. Alspach, eds. *The Variorum Edition of the Poems of W. B. Yeats.* London: Macmillan, 1957.

VPl   Alspach, R. K., ed. *The Variorum Edition of the Plays of W. B. Yeats.* London: Macmillan, 1966.

Preface

W. B. Yeats spent a great deal of his life immersing himself in magical, mystical, and philosophical studies in order, as he claimed, to devise a personal system of thought "that would leave [his] . . . imagination free to create as it chose and yet make all that it created, or could create, part of the one history, and that the soul's" (*AV* (A) xi). While he set down much of the ensuing system in a series of philosophical treatises culminating in *A Vision* and in what is perhaps the most succinct statement of his philosophy, "The Seven Propositions" of 1937, this same system infiltrates, at times overtly, but more often covertly, virtually all of his plays.

Yeats wrote of his first published play that "If I had not made magic my constant study . . . *The Countess Kathleen* [could not] have ever come to exist" (*L* 211), and of his last play, *The Death of Cuchulain*, that "my 'private philosophy' is there but there must be no sign of it; all must be like an old faery tale" (*L* 917). Similar references to the "magical," "mystical," "religious," or "philosophical" beliefs which permeate his plays can be found scattered throughout Yeats's letters, the notes to the plays, and many of his essays. Yeats described *The Shadowy Waters* in 1897 as "magical and mystical beyond anything I have done" (*L* 280), while he said of *The Herne's Egg* in 1935 that "Shri Purohit Swami is with me, and the play is his philosophy in a fable, or mine confirmed by him" (*DWL* 46), and of *Purgatory* in 1938 that "I have put nothing into the play that seemed picturesque; I have put there my own convictions about this world and the next" (*DWL* 202). The Unicorn, a central character in two of Yeats's plays, is "a private symbol belonging to my mystical order" (*L* 662); *The Cat and the Moon* is composed of "incidents and metaphors that are related to certain beliefs of mine as are the patterns upon a Persian carpet to some ancient faith or philosophy" (*VP1* 805). Moreover, while Yeats struggled for over twenty years to remove philosophical abstractions from *The Player Queen*, he nevertheless wrote rather proudly of *The Herne's Egg* that it has more "philosophic depth" than the former play (*DWL* 43).

A study of Yeats's "private philosophy" as it is developed in his drama is warranted on the basis of these statements alone. The need for such a study is underscored by Yeats's obsession with both orthodox and unorthodox systems of belief throughout his life, an obsession which was strong enough to disrupt the writing of several plays, and which brought his dramatic work to a virtual standstill for long periods of his life. Yeats the dramatist and Yeats the metaphysician are in fact virtually inseparable. It was while writing *The Player Queen* that Yeats developed the theory of opposites which would figure prominently in *A Vision*; a rehearsal of *At the Hawk's Well* inspired him to begin his first long philosophical treatise, "Per Amica Silentia Lunae." Conversely, the "religious" or "mystical" or "philosophic" beliefs which Yeats espoused shape most of the plays.

Much of Yeats's voluminous body of dramatic theory underscores his belief in a necessary relationship between drama and religion. As is well known, Yeats deplored the widespread acceptance at the end of the nineteenth century of the scientific (rationalistic) explanation of life which negated the spiritual life, not only in other worlds, but in this world, and within human beings themselves. He was especially concerned with the degree to which this world view permeated even the arts, and often reiterated that the sterility of modern art in general, and of modern drama in particular, was due to its divorce from myth and religion. Yeats wished to reunite art and religion, and particularly drama and religion, as George M. Harper has noted in his study of Yeats's dramatic theory, "The Mingling of Heaven and Earth":

"The more religious the subject-matter of an art," he wrote, "the more will it be as it were, stationary, and the more ancient will be the emotion that it arouses and the circumstance that it calls up before our eyes." Such arguments for art as religion are the basis of Yeats's symbolic aesthetic.[1]

At the same time, Yeats could not bring himself to espouse traditional religious beliefs, though he toyed with Catholicism and Hinduism for brief periods of his life. He therefore set two main goals for himself – to discover a coherent religious or philosophical system that he could wholeheartedly believe in, and at the same time to develop an art form that would breathe life into this system. He particularly wanted to create a form of drama that would incorporate his religious beliefs not only into the words and lyrics, but into the very movement

1 George M. Harper, "The Mingling of Heaven and Earth: Yeats's Theory of Theatre," in *New Yeats Papers X* (Dublin: Dolmen Press, 1975), pp. 17-18.

and ritual of the plays. Yeats experimented with various dramatic forms in his long career as a playwright, trying to write "modern mystery plays" (*L* 280), but the most successful blending of belief and structure occurs in his dance plays. These dance plays are strikingly similar, as has often been noted, to the Japanese Noh plays, but their similarity is almost completely coincidental, a result of their similar world view. Yeats embraced the Japanese plays when he was introduced to them, because they provided him with an established tradition for his own dramatic experiments, and thus gave him greater confidence in them, but these plays actually influenced the development of Yeats's drama far less than is often supposed. It can be argued, as Virginia Moore did as early as 1954,[2] that the plays are at least as indebted to the dramatic rituals of magic used by the esoteric order of the Golden Dawn which Yeats joined in 1890, and to the rituals for a Celtic magical order which he and a number of Golden Dawn members spent several years devising around the turn of the century.

In addition to finding a suitable form for his plays, Yeats also struggled to translate the abstractions of his philosophical system into a coherent symbolism. As a poet, he firmly believed that age-old symbols were best suited for transmitting the deepest truths. At the same time, his plays often began their life full of abstract language and metaphysical argument, and he had to revise them over and over again, gradually replacing argument with symbolism. This constant revision had two results. At their most successful, Yeats's plays breathe life and meaning into the dry and often abstruse statements of *A Vision* and "The Seven Propositions" (cf. p. 17). But, because the philosophical treatises are usually more logically ordered, many subtle, even obscure passages in the plays are more readily understandable when studied together with the philosophical works.

It is therefore my intention to trace "the history of the soul" or spirit as it is developed through Yeats's plays, while drawing attention, whenever necessary, to the philosophical treatises.[3] I do not pretend to pursue all the ramifications of all the tenets of Yeats's system, nor can I hope to unearth all the ways in which it infiltrates the drama. I intend only to elucidate the underlying system of beliefs and to establish its relation to the aim and execution of the plays by tracing and explicating a few of the themes, metaphors, and symbols through which it is

---

2 Virginia Moore, *The Unicorn: William Butler Yeats's Search for Reality* (New York: Macmillan, 1954), pp. 27, 73-83.

3 These will include the manuscript notes and rituals for Yeats's proposed Celtic magical order which have been edited by Lucy Kalogera in her Ph.D. dissertation "Yeats's Celtic Mysteries" (Florida State University, 1977), and which will be referred to in the text as *CMK*.

developed in the drama. I have focused on the verbal content of the plays in this study, though there is little doubt that Yeats's beliefs were equally instrumental in shaping their form and structure.

I have found the manuscript versions and the earliest published versions of the plays to be indispensable to this study, since they often retain much of the abstract thought which Yeats eliminated from the later versions, and also show the development of the metaphors and images with which Yeats gradually replaced it.[4] I have grouped the plays by theme, without very much regard to chronology except as this is dictated by the themes within the plays themselves. The impossibility of studying the plays in any meaningful chronological way has often been pointed out; Yeats rewrote and revised his plays far too often. As he himself wrote in the "Preface" to *Poems: 1899-1905*, "I have printed the plays and poems in the order of their first publication, but so far as the actual writing of verse is concerned, *The Shadowy Waters* and *On Baile's Strand* have been so much rewritten that they are later than *The King's Threshold*."[5]

I have also underplayed chronology because my aim has been not so much to emphasize the development of Yeats's ideas as to stress the continuity of thought from one play to another, from the earliest manuscript versions of *The Shadowy Waters* to *The Death of Cuchulain*. A close study of Yeats's drama reveals that he held his most profound beliefs about the nature and history of the spirit at an early age. Studied as a unit, the plays reveal in practice the system that the philosophical treatises expound in theory; indeed, much of the excitement for me has come from seeing, through the plays, just *how* his system works. The same metaphors and symbols, and even, at times, the same words and phrases are used from one play to another, and all explicate the same underlying story.

Yeats often declared that he was molding his beliefs into a cohesive system of thought, a system which, though he believed in it as an independent body of knowledge, would also provide him with "metaphors for poetry" (*AV* (B) 8). Yeats alternated between calling this system his "religious system" and his "private philosophy"; the terms are interchangeable since for him both disciplines have in common their central preoccupation with the nature of the soul or spirit. For my purposes it is simplest to label it a metaphysics.

4 Yeats was a notoriously poor speller. The manuscripts quoted from in this book display a characteristic disregard for the niceties of spelling and punctuation.
5 Quoted by S. B. Bushrui, *Yeats's Verse Plays: The Revisions 1900-1910* (Oxford: Clarendon Press, 1965), pp. xiv-xv.

1

"Metaphors for Poetry"

The Metaphysician

It was in search of a coherent, but personal, metaphysics that, Yeats tells us, he began his study of esoteric traditions in the 1880s: "Some were looking for spiritual happiness or for some form of unknown power, but I had a practical object. I wished for a system of thought that would leave my imagination free to create as it chose and yet make all that it created, or could create, part of the one history, and that the soul's" (*AV* (A) xi). Yeats's youthful fascination first with Theosophy and the teachings of Mme Blavatsky and then with the theory and practice of magic through MacGregor Mathers and others is well documented, not least in his own writing, the clearest example of which is his unfinished novel, *The Speckled Bird*. Writes William Murphy, "Readers of . . . that intense, astonishingly personal autobiographical novel . . . will understand and appreciate the depth, earnestness and sincerity of the poet's devotion to the occult."[1]

Yeats became a serious student of the occult, of magic, mysticism, and spiritism, and he pursued this study until late in life. He was very active in the inner circles of Theosophy until he fell into disfavour with Mme Blavatsky for advocating the study of practical magic in the Esoteric Section, the study group to which he belonged. He then joined the magical Order of the Golden Dawn, founded by master masons including his magical mentor MacGregor Mathers, and became an extraordinarily active member, as is exhaustively documented in G. M. Harper's *Yeats' Golden Dawn*.[2] Yeats held the post of Instructor of Mystical Philosophy for years, and was a key figure in the restructur-

---

1 In G. M. Harper, ed., *Yeats and the Occult* (Toronto: Macmillan of Canada, 1975), p. 25.
2 G. M. Harper, *Yeats's Golden Dawn* (New York: Barnes & Noble, 1974), pp. 80, 30, 181, and elsewhere.

ing of the order after the painful break with Mathers in 1900. Yeats belonged to the Golden Dawn and to its successor the Order of the Stella Matutina for thirty-two years. In addition, he was an Associate Member of the Society of Psychical Research from 1913 to 1928.[3]

Yeats took his esoteric studies very seriously; they were inextricably intertwined with his literary activities, and he insisted on proclaiming them publicly while "enduring unbelief and misbelief and ridicule as best one may" (EI 38). He made no apologies for them, since it was often while pursuing these studies that he found his muse. As he wrote in A Vision, "Muses resemble women who creep out at night and give themselves to unknown sailors and return to talk of Chinese porcelain . . . or of the Ninth Symphony – virginity renews itself like the moon – except that the Muses sometimes form in these low haunts their most lasting attachments" (AV (B) 24). His essay entitled "Magic," a manifesto of sorts, begins, "I believe in the practice and philosophy of what we have agreed to call magic, in what I must call the evocation of spirits, though I do not know what they are, in the power of creating magical illusions, in the visions of truth in the depths of the mind when the eyes are closed . . ." (EI 28). What Yeats is referring to is ritual magic, a rigorous spiritual and scientific discipline combined with a transcendental doctrine which teaches that human beings are one with nature and one with the gods. The magical order of the Golden Dawn combined studies of the ancient wisdom tradition, including Rosicrucian lore and the Kabbalah, with astrology and the tarot, and turned the whole into a system of practical magic which allowed the initiate (in theory at any rate, though Yeats's writings indicate that he achieved a measure of success), through dedication and practice, to leave the physical body through astral travel and even, through skrying (travelling directly to higher planes of existence) and divination, to converse with the gods. The aims of the order are reflected in the "Obligations of an Adeptus Minor":

I further solemnly swear that with the Divine permission, I will from this day forward apply myself unto the Great Work, which is to purify and exalt my Spiritual Nature, that with the Divine aid, I may at length attain to be *more than human*, and thus gradually raise and unify myself to my *Higher and Divine Genius* and that in this [unreadable word] I will not abuse the Great Power entrusted unto me.[4]

3 G. M. Harper, "Editorial Introduction," in *A Critical Edition of* A Vision *(1925)* (London: Macmillan, 1978), p. xi.
4 From the Adeptus Minor Ritual written in Yeats's own hand, Yeats's papers, Reel 11, vol. 3, pp. 75-76, The William Butler Archives, Center for Contemporary Arts and Letters, State University of New York at Stony Brook.

Israel Regardie, a fellow member of the Golden Dawn and a prolific demystifier of magic, writes of the magician that,

His is the task, and his alone, of transforming the universe, and of transmuting the base elements of matter into the substance of the veritable spirit. A constant alchemical operation must the whole of his life become, during which he distills in the alembic of his heart the grossness of the world into the essence of the cloudless skies.[5]

Yeats used magic in this way, not as a means of acquiring temporal power, but as a key to a higher spiritual life. Traditional magic, along with Theosophy and spiritism, was for him a means of rediscovering the spiritual and imaginative truths which he felt had been understood in ancient times and still were by the uneducated classes such as the Irish peasantry and the servant girls of Soho, but which were largely lost in the modern world through an overemphasis on the mind and the rational faculties. Yeats spent his life trying to understand the nature of the spirit, and welcomed any opportunity to glimpse another facet of it. For this reason he immersed himself in various studies, such as magic and spiritism, which even in occult circles were considered incompatible;[6] "I was comparing one form of belief with another, and like Paracelsus, who claimed to have collected his knowledge from midwife and hangman, I was discovering a philosophy" (*VB* 311).

Yeats studied these disciplines carefully, but he did not swallow all their tenets whole, and could laugh at the follies and excesses of each. While still an active Theosophist, for example, Yeats wrote to Katherine Tynan about "a sad accident [which] happened at Madame Blavatsky's lately, I hear. A big materialist sat on the astral double of a poor young Indian. It was sitting on the sofa and he was too material to be able to see it. Certainly a sad accident!" (*L* 59). Throughout even the obsessive *The Speckled Bird*, which he wrote while he was still trying to create a Celtic magical order, Yeats poked gentle fun at the fanatics and middle-class eccentrics he met in occult circles. This sense of humour, coupled with a healthy skepticism, is very much in evidence throughout his work, and is an important part even of *A Vision* which, as H. Adams has pointed out, is much more tongue-in-cheek than is generally acknowledged.[7] A balance of belief and skepticism is also

5 I. Regardie, *The Tree of Life: A Study of Magic* (New York: Samuel Weiser, 1969), pp. 233-34.

6 Spiritists consider magic to be fantastic and superstitious, while magicians dismiss spiritism as a passive practice which deals with the lower astral plane, "the region of Qliphotic shells and demons and decaying phantasms of the dead," instead of with higher spiritual forces (Regardie, *Tree of Life*, p. 153).

7 H. Adams, "Some Yeatsian Versions of Comedy," in N. Jeffares, ed., *In Excited Reverie* (New York: Macmillan, 1965), pp. 152-70.

evident in the plays, notably in the highly esoteric, but equally irreverent, *The Herne's Egg*.

Yeats's metaphysics is in fact considerably more orthodox than his preoccupation with the occult would lead us to believe. To begin with, the Western philosophic tradition has very strong ties with the occult tradition which was resurfacing at the turn of the century in Europe, and in which Yeats was immersing himself. As James Olney argues, "Going back to Plato himself, and even earlier to Pythagoras and Empedocles, the exoteric tradition had its counterpart in a parallel esoteric tradition; and point by point along their parallel paths the philosophy offered justification for that other darker brother."[8] Yeats's philosophy can in many instances be traced both to occult sources such as Mme Blavatsky's books or Golden Dawn tenets and to exoteric philosophic works – on many points these traditions are virtually interchangeable.[9]

Yeats absorbed a great deal of exoteric philosophy indirectly, through his occult studies and through poets such as Shelley, Coleridge, and Blake, but he also devoted a considerable amount of time to the study of Eastern and Western philosophies. He became acquainted with the former early in life, through his contacts with the India-based Theosophical Society, with Mohini Chatterjee and his friend AE (George Russell), and with the Indian dramatist Tagore. This interest was rekindled in the last few years of his life by his friendship with the Indian monk Shri Purohit Swami, with whom he translated *The Ten Principal Upanishads*. Yeats's interests in Western philosophy took longer to develop, since he was so skeptical in his youth of the value of logical, abstract thought, equating it, like Blake, with a dearth of holiness (*VB* 20). Nevertheless, following the publishing of the first version of *A Vision*, a decidedly abstract work (though Yeats at first tried to clothe it in myth), he began to read Western philosophy seriously, and spent the ten years between 1925 and 1935 studying it "chiefly to test *A Vision*."[10] As Yeats explained to T. Sturge Moore in 1926,

When it [*A Vision*] was written . . . I started to read. I read for months every day Plato and Plotinus. Then I started on Berkeley and Croce and Gentile. You introduced me to your brother [the realist George Moore]'s work and to

8 James Olney, "Yeats and Jung," in Harper, ed., *Yeats and the Occult*, p. 29.

9 Olney points out in "Yeats and Jung," pp. 38-39, that "Plotinus, who did not practice magic but who 'Believed in it,' provided the philosophic bridge between Plato and the Neoplatonic theurgists in his explanation of how magic works" in the Fourth Ennead, Tractate 4, no. 40.

10 Virginia Moore, *The Unicorn: William Butler Yeats's Search for Reality* (New York: Macmillan, 1954), p. 27.

[Bertrand] Russell, and I found Eddington and one or two others for myself. I am still however anything but at my ease in recent philosophy. I find your brother extraordinarily obscure.

(*TSML* 83)

He persevered, with boundless enthusiasm and increasing confidence, as his long philosophical correspondence with T. S. Moore attests. Besides consistently pointing out flaws in the realist George Moore's arguments, he also began to rail against Bertrand Russell, whose work he was "reading daily" (*TSML* 115), and whom he immortalized in the correspondence as "the Bald One":

You say Bertrand Russell says Kant smashed his own philosophy by his doctrine of practical reason. So he does say, and what more can you expect from a man who has been entirely bald during the whole course of his life. He merely repeats a piece of common electioneering nonsense which writer has copied from writer for generations. The men who invented it had as much to do with philosophy as an Orange brass band on the twelfth of July has to do with religion.

(*TSML* 124)[11]

He began to read widely in the Western philosophic tradition, studying "chronologically, Heraclitus, Pythagoras, Empedocles, Plato, Plotinus, Nicholas of Cusa, the Cambridge Platonists, Berkeley, the German and Italian idealists, Whitehead, and McTaggart"[12] and the influence of this study is felt repeatedly in the 1937 edition of *A Vision*.

Yeats immersed himself in these diverse schools of thought with a specific purpose in mind: to mold a personal metaphysics, a personal "system of thought." It is my contention that he succeeded in developing a coherent and cohesive metaphysics. While it is original only if, in Kathleen Raine's words, "by original we mean a return to the origins of knowledge which have been discovered and known again and again, and as often lost and forgotten,"[13] it is a synthesis of those traditions which corroborated his own fledgling beliefs. With the exception of Raine and a handful of others, there was until recently little support for

11 While Yeats's sense of humour is very much in evidence in these letters, he was nevertheless in earnest. Thus he wrote of Russell in 1927, "I am reading that bald-pate daily. When I read him before I knew little, but now for 4 years I have read nothing but philosophy and I understand what has happened. The scientific and psychological parts are amazingly accurate, but as for the philosophy – the bald-pate sprouts radishes" (*TSML* 115).

12 Moore, *The Unicorn*, p. 344. For a detailed discussion of the thought of the earliest of these philosophers, and of the parallel between their thought and Yeats's, cf. James Olney, *The Rhizome and the Flower: The Perennial Philosophy – Yeats and Jung* (Berkeley: University of California Press, 1980).

13 Kathleen Raine, "Hades Wrapped in Cloud," in Harper, ed., *Yeats and the Occult*, p. 104.

this conclusion among Yeats scholars, many of whom have assumed, with T. Sturge Moore, that whatever his other merits, Yeats was not much of a thinker. This has changed considerably with the publication of James Olney's important book *The Rhizome and the Flower*, which underscores Yeats's significance as a thinker, and his philosophical ties to C. G. Jung and to the great pre-Platonic and neo-Platonic traditions.

Yeats welcomed the various traditions that came his way, for he wanted to feel himself in the mainstream of thought: to feel that he was historically right, and not just reacting to a past age. As he wrote to T. Sturge Moore, "I feel that an imaginative writer whose work draws him to philosophy must attach himself to some great historic school. My dreams and much psychic phenomena force me into a certain little-trodden way but I must not go too far from the main European track" (*TSML* 149). This desire for tradition was fueled not so much by a lack of confidence in his own ideas (though there was an element of that in his early years) as by his belief that if his ideas were true they would not be original to him, but would be received from the world soul, ancient truths enshrined in the oldest religious and philosophic traditions and in the work of the most venerable of poets. This belief is evident even in the more self-serving statements of his later life, such as the following description of the work of many of his contemporaries:

These new men are goldsmiths working with a glass screwed into one eye, while we stride ahead of the crowd, its swordsmen, its jugglers, looking to right and left. "To right and left" by which I mean that we need like Milton, Shakespeare, Shelley, vast sentiments, generalizations supported by tradition.

(*DWL* 64-65)

Nevertheless, though Yeats took pains to explore all the systems of belief which he came across, there is considerable evidence in his work that he assimilated only those traditions which confirmed and elaborated the beliefs which he intuited as a young man. Yeats claimed in his *Memoirs* that he held his most important ideas by the age of twenty, though he lacked the words and the confidence with which to express them, just as, in his essay "The Philosophy of Shelley's Poetry," he claimed the same for Shelley. Speaking of *Queen Mab*, he wrote that it "was written before he [Shelley] had found his deepest thought, or rather perhaps before he had found words to utter it, for I do not think men change much in their deepest thought" (*EI* 69). Though Yeats was elated when he found a school or tradition which confirmed one or another of his beliefs, no single one ever changed his work radically. More often than not its tenets are to be found in his writing long before he was exposed to the tradition which supposedly revolutionized his work. Indeed, considering that Yeats devoted so much time to studying the tenets of such diverse traditions, the continuity of thought in his work is quite remarkable.

Long before Yeats encountered structured occult schools he had devised, as the *Autobiographies* and letters attest, his own mysticism. Long before he encountered the Noh drama, he had devised a religious drama with stark settings and supernatural characters, using masks and substituting metaphor and symbol for argument. In the letters to AE of 1903 can be found the nucleus of the theory of historical cycles which Yeats later outlined in "Per Amica Silentia Lunae," while in "Per Amica" can be found the nucleus of the argument that Yeats's communicators would elaborate in *A Vision*. And while "The Seven Propositions" of 1937 indicate, as Richard Ellmann has suggested, that "during his last decade he [Yeats] pushed his speculations about final matters even further,"[14] the propositions are on most counts an elaboration, or an authoritative restatement, of his long-held beliefs on the nature of being.

In his "Dedication" to the 1925 edition of *A Vision*, Yeats wrote that this was the system of belief that he had long been looking for. But though he claimed that it had only now come to him "though it may be too late" (*AV* (A) xi), there is more than enough evidence in the body of his work to support the argument that this system, in its essence if not in all its particulars, is present in a recognizable form in the earliest works. This is also James Olney's argument in *The Rhizome and the Flower*; he writes that Yeats "was as system-minded in 1893 as in 1933, and . . . there is an astonishing amount of *A Vision* already present in the commentary on 'The Symbolic System' in *The Works of William Blake*."[15]

Yeats's drama provides evidence that Yeats was system-minded from the outset. Even the earliest manuscript versions of *The Shadowy Waters*, written in the 1880s, transmit, often with startling clarity, a metaphysics which is consistent with, and even at times sheds light on, that set down in such later philosophical treatises as "Per Amica Silentia Lunae" and *A Vision*. This is stressed by the editors of these manuscript versions, who note that they "reveal another part of the still largely hidden foundation in mythology and occultism on which rests the works of the Yeats we know"; here one finds, they continue, "the first appearance of ideas and images which also preoccupy the later Yeats" (*DrC* xv).

14 Richard Ellmann, "At the Yeatses," *New York Review of Books*, May 17, 1979, p. 23.
15 Olney, *The Rhizome and the Flower*, p. 349.

The Metaphysician versus the Dramatist

Granted, then, that Yeats developed a metaphysics which infiltrates all the work, early as well as late, one to which he draws attention time and time again, we are now faced with the problem of how to study the systematic thought of a man who long railed against abstract thought in general and "complete ideas" (*Memoirs* 165) in particular, and sought to obscure his system almost as often as he sought to demystify it. The problem arises because Yeats seems to have been torn by two conflicting impulses. The first, a product of his skeptical, inquiring mind, was to understand the meaning of existence and the relationship of spirit to matter in a rational way, to devise a system of thought that would be "an ancient discipline, a philosophy that satisfied the intellect" (*EI* 429). The second impulse, fed by his revulsion at "an Irish Protestant point of view that suggested by its blank abstraction chloride of lime" (*EI* 428), was to abandon all dogma, all abstraction, and to strive for irrational, unnamable, intuitive "truth." Yeats stated his dilemma succintly in *A Vision*: "Having the concrete mind of a poet, I am unhappy when I find myself among abstract things, and yet I need them to set my experiences in order" (*AV* (A) 129).

Yeats's prose writings throughout his career emphasize the need to abandon the speculations of science and metaphysics for *passion*, for the truth of the heart rather than the intellect (*EI* 265). In this belief Yeats was clearly at the forefront of his time. Introducing what became one of Yeats's favourite books, *The Secret of the Golden Flower*, C. G. Jung wrote in 1931 that "the reaction which is now beginning in the West against the intellect in favour of feeling, or in favour of intuition, seems to me a mark of cultural advance, a widening of consciousness beyond the too narrow limits of a tyrannical intellect."[16] Yeats believed that the poet, and not the philosopher, must now assume the mantle forfeited by an overly rational church. Poetry transforms philosophy, clothing it with flesh and blood and removing it from the deadening level of abstraction: "Art bids us touch and taste and hear and see the world, and shrinks from what Blake calls mathematical form, from every abstract thing, from all that is of the brain only, from all that is not a fountain jetting from the entire hopes, memories and sensations of the body" (*EI* 292-93). At the same time, through symbols, through intuitive flights of the imagination rather than through logically ordered thought, it can reach further, grasp deeper meanings than those available to the intellect. Thus the use of art to transform philosophy is twofold: while it makes the thought more concrete and therefore more

16 C. G. Jung, "European Commentary," in *The Secret of the Golden Flower*, trans. C. F. Barnes (New York: Harcourt, Brace, 1931), p. 85.

accessible, it also frees it from the bonds of reason that keep the spirit from grasping greater truths.

> The more a poet rids his verses of heterogeneous knowledge and irrelevant analysis, and purifies his mind with elaborate art, the more does the little ritual of his verse resemble the great ritual of Nature, and becomes mysterious and inscrutable. He becomes, as all the great mystics have believed, a vessel of the creative power of God; and whether he be a great poet or a small poet, we can praise the poems, which but seem to be his, with the extremity of praise that we give this great ritual which is but copied from the same eternal model.
>
> (*EI* 201-202)

These were noble sentiments, but very difficult to follow in practice, and increasingly so as Yeats continued to amass "heterogeneous knowledge." The religious system had to be mulled over, the revelations exulted over, and this took up an increasingly large portion of Yeats's thoughts. Though he struggled to keep the abstractions of the developing system out of the poetical works, Yeats was not always successful; the abstractions continued to infiltrate the poetic works and even, as during the writing of *The Player Queen*, to displace the poetry altogether. As he wrote following his experience with *The Player Queen*, "I find that my philosophical tendency spoils my playwriting if I have not a separate channel for it" (*L* 533). Yeats's solution was to write down the system separately, as an abstract body of thought, and at the same time to rewrite the poetical works to remove as much of the *overt* philosophy as possible.

Yeats increasingly devoted as much attention to these "separate channels" as to his poetic work. The philosophical essays such as "Per Amica Silentia Lunae," the two versions of *A Vision*, "The Seven Propositions," Yeats's letters to T. Sturge Moore, Dorothy Wellesley, and others, and, when they are finally published, his massive and carefully kept records of spiritual and occult experiments, all testify to his need to set down, in abstract, rational terms, his emerging system of thought.

"Per Amica Silentia Lunae," published in 1918, and divided into "Anima Hominis," the human soul, and "Anima Mundi," the soul of the world, represents Yeats's first serious attempt to describe his understanding of such key philosophical concepts as historical cycles, the cycles of life and death, free-will and determinism, and the relationship of human beings to their fate, in alternate terms one's daimon or guardian angel, that being loved and hated the most. These concepts are central to Yeats's system, and infuse virtually all of his work. "Per Amica" is particularly useful as a gloss on the plays, since these feature every conceivable relationship between a man (or woman) and his/her daimon, and dramatize many of the philosophical issues raised in the essay. It is also useful as a gloss on the much more difficult *A Vision*.

A Vision is crucial to an understanding of Yeats's metaphysics. It is at first difficult to place in the canon of Yeats's work, since he claimed in 1925 that it was based on an ancient Arabic manuscript written by one Giraldus in the sixteenth century, of which he was merely the editor, and later, more truthfully, that it was based on scripts of automatic handwriting that certain disembodied "communicators" had dictated to him through his wife. These scripts do exist, and it now seems indisputable that the genesis of *A Vision* was in fact these sessions of automatic handwriting. Nevertheless, as Yeats acknowledged, many of the themes developed in *A Vision* are his own:

> The unknown writer [the "communicators" of *A Vision*] took his theme at first from my just published *Per Amica Silentia Lunae*. I had made a distinction between the perfection that is from a man's combat with himself and that which is from a combat with circumstance, and upon this simple distinction he built up an elaborate classification of men according to their more or less complete expression of one type or the other. He supported his classification by a series of geometrical symbols and put these symbols in an order that answered the question in my essay as to whether some prophet could not prick upon the calendar the birth of a Napoleon or a Christ. . . . Sometimes when my mind strays back to those first days I remember that Browning's Paracelsus did not obtain the secret until he had written his spiritual history at the bidding of his Byzantine teacher, that before initiation Wilhelm Meister read his own history written by another, and I compare my *Per Amica* to those histories.
>
> (*AV* (B) 8-9)

Yeats reworked these scripts for the 1925 edition and then, much more extensively, for the 1937 edition of *A Vision*, explicating the most abstract concepts, in particular the elaborate geometric symbols, adding layers of myth and tying it all in to his own system. The result is a difficult but intriguing and often beautiful work which Yeats made his own, and which at times echoes, at other times illuminates, the rest of his writing. *A Vision* explains the world on three levels: the individual (explaining human character), the historical (providing for a cyclical theory of history), and the cosmological (explaining the relationship between humanity and the cosmos, between the world of time and eternity).[17] Though these levels are contiguous, the individual level is elaborated in the most detail in "The Great Wheel" chapter of *A Vision* and in "The Phases of the Moon," the historical in "The Great Year of the Ancients" and "Dove or Swan," and the cosmological in "The Completed Symbol" and "The Soul in Judgment."

17 My thanks to Shirley Neumann for pointing out these three levels to me.

Yeats was a keen astrologer for most of his life, as even a cursory examination of his letters and private papers makes evident. He was always conscious of the effect of planetary influences on the individual character, and this interest, which permeates, however subtly, all of his work, is obviously at the root of the complex theory of lunar phases and their effect on the human character which is developed in "The Great Wheel" chapter of *A Vision*. At the same time, Yeats was greatly excited by the details which his communicators provided of the twenty-eight lunar phases, or lives, through which the individual soul must pass before being liberated from the wheel of time, and this excitement spilled over into his dramatic and poetic work, and in particular into the writing of *The Only Jealousy of Emer*.

The exposition by Yeats's communicators of the theory of lunar phases was completed in November 1917, while Yeats completed the first version of *The Only Jealousy of Emer* in January of 1918 (*L* 645). The importance of "The Great Wheel" to *The Only Jealousy* has long been noted by Yeats scholars such as Helen Vendler, Leonard Nathan, and F. A. C. Wilson, who have spent a considerable amount of space identifying the phases to which each of the characters in this and other plays belong. Interestingly enough, Yeats's *The Player Queen*, which was largely completed *before* the dictation of *A Vision* began, also concentrates, more than any other play except *The Only Jealousy*, on the effect of the horoscope on human personality. Because Yeats's theory of lunar phases is well known, and its influence on his plays well documented, I have spent relatively little time exploring it in this study; it is simply an alternate metaphor for the struggle between human beings and their fate (if they resist) or their destiny (if they choose not to resist) which is one of Yeats's most enduring themes (cf. ch. 4).

A Vision's alternating historical cycles, each succeeding the other approximately every two thousand years, each living the other's death, dying the other's life, also have their roots in Yeats's early concerns; they can be understood as Yeats's astrological beliefs played out on a larger scale. Yeats, MacGregor Mathers, and their fellow occultists had been expecting a dramatic reversal of historical cycles around the turn of the century similar to the reversal brought about by Jesus Christ, whose birth and death, Yeats believed, signalled the end of an *antithetical* age and the beginning of a new *primary* age. Yeats never wavered in his belief that a new *antithetical* age was about to begin, though he could complain with Septimus in *The Player Queen* that it was slow in coming: "Gather about me, for I announce the end of the Christian Era, the coming of a New Dispensation, that of the New

Adam, that of the Unicorn; but alas, he is chaste, he hesitates, he hesitates" (*MPQ* 421). Yeats identified these reversals with great catastrophes, with the destruction of the earth by flood and fire, also symbols, though on a larger scale, of the forces of destiny with which man must battle. These cycles will be discussed in greater detail in Chapter 4, in the context of Yeats's understanding of free-will and determinism.

Yeats seems to have been most pleased by *A Vision*'s development of a cosmology liking mortal to spirit and birth to death. He was particularly pleased with his "The Soul in Judgment" chapter, writing to Ethel Mannin, "I think I have done one good deed [with *A Vision*] in clearing out of the state from death to birth all the infinities and eternities, and picturing a state as 'phenomenal' as that from birth to death. I have constructed a myth, but then one can believe in a myth — one only assents to philosophy" (*L* 781). In this chapter he charted six different states between death and birth, states which are dramatized in a number of his plays.[18] The journey between death and birth is an integral part of Yeats's cosmology, a cosmology which infiltrates his work from early to late and which is particularly important to an understanding of the plays.

Yeats took the system of thought outlined in *A Vision* very seriously. Addressing his fellow students of the occult, he suggested in the "Dedication" to the first edition that "if they will master what is most abstract there and make it the foundation of their visions, the curtain may ring up a new era" (*AV* (A) xii). The disembodied communicators, he believed, had come to offer him a science, and it is undeniable that Yeats would have liked his system, and in particular his "phenomenological" world between life and death, to be researched and accepted. This would be in keeping with his own contribution to such research during his years as an active member of the Society for Psychical Research. He longed for such validation, writing, "Will some mathematician some day question and understand, as I cannot, and confirm all, or have I also [comparing himself to Plato] dealt in myth?" (*AV* (B) 213).

Having written down the abstractions which haunted him, Yeats was free for a time to return to his first loves, poetry and drama. As he wrote following the completion of the first edition of *A Vision*, "I can now, if I have the energy, find the simplicity I have sought in vain. I need no longer write poems like 'The Phases of the Moon' nor 'Ego Dominus Tuus' nor spend barren years, as I have done some three or four times, striving with abstractions that substituted themselves for

18 See Chapters 2 and 3 for a discussion of these states and their importance in the plays.

the play that I had planned" (*AV* (A) xii). Though his philosophy is obviously central to the poetic works, Yeats laboured, through extensive revisions, to remove or subsume all obvious traces of it. He described this process of playwriting in "Estrangement":

At first, if [a play] has psychological depth, there is a bundle of ideas, something that can be stated in philosophical terms; my *Countess Cathleen*, for instance, was once the moral question, may a soul sacrifice itself for a good end? but gradually philosophy is eliminated until at last the only philosophy audible, if there is even that, is the mere expression of one character or another. When it is completely life it seems to the hasty reader a mere story.[19]

This is in keeping with the advice that he gave Margot Ruddock when she was attempting to write a play:

I do not think a play where everyone speaks my thought can be the greatest kind of play no matter how written. Goethe said, "a philosopher needs all his philosophy but must keep it out of his work" (which he could not do). Take some plot which seeks to express all in the action and where nothing is said about the action; do not speak through the characters, let them speak through you, and you will find that at some moment of crisis they will speak at once passionately and profoundly.

(*MRL* 80)

Yeats continued to consider himself primarily a poet and a dramatist, and to believe in the greater power of symbols and myths to transmit "the experience of the soul" (*SB* 206).[20] He perfected his use of symbols, many of them eclectic symbols studied with the magical Order of the Golden Dawn, until he could write after the rehearsals of *At the Hawk's Well*, "I have invented a form of drama, distinguished, indirect, and symbolic" (*EI* 221). Symbols in place, Yeats discarded much of the logic until even he, as he wrote of the symbols in *The Cat and the Moon*, completely forgot (or so he claimed) what they originally stood for: "I have altogether forgotten whether other parts of the fable [on which the play is based] have, as is very likely, a precise meaning, and that is natural, for I generally forget in contemplating my copy of an old Persian carpet that its winding and wandering vine had once that philosophical meaning" (*VP1* 805). Yeats gave this same answer when he was asked the meaning of the Fool and the Blind Man in *On Baile's Strand*, but though it was a convenient excuse he was only half serious. The copious allusions in his prose writings to the metaphysics

---

19 *The Autobiography of W. B. Yeats* (New York: Collier Books, 1965), pp. 316-17.

20 The full passage is of some interest: "Even the speculative writers who would touch the heart should choose their mythology and cycle of legends, for life can only be expressed by life... but not by a doctrine or a speculation or a definition in the reason. These are only useful when they point the way to a sound or an image or an odour or to the experience of the soul when all these become one and nothing."

which informs the drama, and in particular the lengthy prefaces and notes to the plays, not only indicate the extent to which Yeats's beliefs – those beliefs so laboriously set down in the various treatises – inform the work, but also prove that he wanted them to be studied and understood.

Yeats certainly hoped that the underlying beliefs would be grasped by the informed, discerning reader of the plays, if not by the larger audience. As he wrote in his poem "To Ireland in the Coming Times":

> to him who ponders well,
> My rhymes more than their rhyming tell
> Of the dim wisdoms old and deep,
> That god gives unto man in sleep.
> For round about my table go
> The magical powers to and fro.
>
> (*VE* 138)

Referring to the members of his audience in the notes to *The Death of Cuchulain*, Yeats wrote that "They can find my words in the book if they are curious, but we will not thrust our secret upon them" (*VP1* 1010). He left many such words, enough to make possible a far lengthier study of his philosophy as it is expressed in the drama than his own study of the philosophy which informs Shelley's poetry, an essay which clearly sets a precedent for the present study.

The Metaphysics in the Drama

For all his work on *A Vision*, Yeats was never completely satisfied with it. He fretted that he had perhaps "not even dealt . . . with the most important part, for I have said little of sexual love nothing of the souls reality [sic]."[21] While the philosophical treatises are invaluable as a guide to the metaphysics outlined in Yeats's poetical works, it is clearly in the latter, and in particular in the plays, that Yeats most successfully outlined his "private philosophy," his understanding of the "souls reality," and of the meaning and importance of "sexual love." That the plays and philosophical treatises should have the same basic concerns is not surprising since, as we have seen, Yeats spent his life looking for a system of belief that would make all his writing "part of the one history, and that the soul's." Drama, according to the definition he gave in *The United Irishman*, was for him "a picture of the soul of man, and not of his external life," while the original title he gave for the manuscripts which he "edited" and presented to the world as *A Vision*

---

21 From the manuscript draft of the dedication to the 1925 edition of *A Vision*, quoted by Harper in his "Editorial Introduction," p. xlvi.

was "The Way of the Soul Between the Sun and the Moon" (*AV* (A) xix). Nevertheless, it might be argued that, while *A Vision* attempts a comprehensive study of what Yeats took to be the nature and history of the soul, within and outside creation, and in both incarnate and discarnate states, the plays centre on the plight of human protagonists and thus seem to limit their "picture" of the soul to its manifestation in the mortal condition.

In fact, however, the plays supply a considerable amount of information about the soul's reality, and for a very simple reason. Yeats saw no need to divorce the plight of mortals from that of spirits in any other state. He understood creation to be a whole, populated by souls, or spirits, on innumerable levels of being between humanity and the gods, and separated one from the other by the thinnest of veils. All spirits, he believed, are equal, for all are a part of the original unity that was shattered at creation into the innumerable components of the universe. Each spirit must pass at some stage of development through all states of being, must be both god and human being.

The plays present a bewildering array of gods, discarnate spirits, half-gods, and mortals, all of whom interact, and in very significant ways. Most mortal protagonists know themselves to be spirits temporarily residing in human form; many long to shed the mortal body even as some discarnate spirits who were once human beings lament the loss of theirs. Gods in some plays bend mortals and lesser spirits to their will, while in other plays mortals, by defying the will of the gods or even, in some cases, by subjugating these gods, become gods themselves. Yeats therefore clearly repudiates in the plays that philosophical position which equates human beings with their mortal condition and which negates both their connection with all other states of being and their ultimate identification with the highest God, or the One. The belief in a hierarchy of being proceeding from humanity to God, and connecting all beings within creation, permeates the drama and is a central tenet of Yeats's metaphysics. Yeats argued, quite seriously, that a major controversy of the time, the contradiction between the realist and idealist philosophical positions, would be resolved were other modern philosophers to espouse this doctrine. As he wrote to Joseph Hone,

I think that much of the confusion of modern philosophy, perhaps the whole realism versus idealism quarrel, comes from our renouncing the ancient hierarchy of beings from man up to the One. What I do not see but may see or have seen, is perceived by another being. In other words is part of the fabric of another being. I remember what he forgets, he remembers what I forget. We are in the midst of life and there is nothing but life.

(*L* 728)

Yeats claimed in his correspondence with T. S. Moore to be both a realist and an idealist, giving as his reason that he saw "no final contradiction" (*TSML* 99) between the two. As Yeats understood it, realists believe that the external world is objective, and therefore permanent, while idealists believe that it is subjective, and therefore only exists or seems to exist while it is being perceived. The difficulty facing the idealists is how to explain the fact that much of this external world can be proven to remain the same no matter when or by whom it is perceived. Berkeley, whom Yeats called "idealist and realist alike," solved this problem by claiming that not only the human mind, but God himself continually perceives, and therefore creates, a stable universe. T. S. Moore was somewhat disdainful of this explanation, and dared Yeats to find a better one: "Berkeley had to resort to God to explain objective reality; God went on thinking and so his thoughts remained just as the objective reality does . . . you must find a definition that, unlike Berkeley's, is not merely verbally different from the view that calls one subjective and the other objective" (*TSML* 78-80). Replied Yeats, "The essential sentence is of course 'things only exist in being perceived,' and I can only call perception God's when I add Blake's 'God only acts or is in existing beings or men'" (*TSML* 80). Yeats continued this argument in his essay "Bishop Berkeley," where he stated that the Berkeley of the *Commonplace Book* seems to posit a hierarchy of being connecting God's act of creation with that of human beings:

he thought of God as a pure indivisible act, personal because at once will and understanding, which unlike the Pure Act of Italian philosophy creates passive "ideas" – sensations – thrusts them as it were outside itself; and in this act all beings – from the hierarchy of Heaven to man and woman and doubtless to all that lives – share in the measure of their worth.

(*EI* 408)

What Yeats is arguing is that, since perception is creation, the external universe is constant as long as it is perceived by one or another of the beings who make up the hierarchy between God and humanity. The question then is not whether it is a human being or God who perceives and thus creates the universe; all aspects of the external universe are perceived by beings on different levels of existence at all times during creation. The statement that "God only acts or is in existing beings or men" adds another dimension to the argument. All beings within creation are separate but equal, and together they form reality. God is simply one of many names for the unity of all things before creation, a complete and undifferentiated unity or emptiness out of which, at creation, stream the spirits who, being separate, perceive each other and thus create "reality." The emptiness or unity may be called God, but it is outside creation, and therefore neither "is" nor "acts" — this is reserved for the diverse spirits who make up, and therefore in some senses equal, the one God outside of time.[22]

These beliefs are most succinctly, if rather cryptically, expressed in Yeats's "The Seven Propositions," written in 1937, in which he outlined what he understood to be the nature of reality *after* creation. Since these propositions will be referred to several times during the course of this study, I shall digress from my argument momentarily in order to print them in their entirety:

(I) Reality is a timeless and spaceless community of Spirits which perceive each other. Each Spirit is determined by and determines those it perceives, and each Spirit is unique.

(II) When these Spirits reflect themselves in time and space they still determine each other, and each Spirit sees the others as thoughts, images, objects of sense. Time and space are unreal.

(III) This reflection into time and space is only complete at certain moments of birth, or passivity, which recur many times in each destiny. At these moments the destiny receives its character until the next such moment from those Spirits who constitute the external universe. The horoscope is a set of geometrical relations between the Spirit's reflection and the principal masses in the universe and defines that character.

(IV) The emotional character of a timeless and spaceless Spirit reflects itself as its position in time, its intellectual character as its position in space. The position of a Spirit in space and time therefore defines character.

(V) Human life is either the struggle of a destiny against all other destinies, or a transformation of the character defined in the horoscope into timeless and spaceless existence. The whole passage from birth to birth should be an epitome of the whole passage of the universe through time and back into its timeless and spaceless condition.

(VI) The acts and nature of a Spirit during any one life are a section or abstraction of reality and are unhappy because incomplete. They are a gyre or part of a gyre, whereas reality is a sphere.

(VII) Though the Spirits are determined by each other they cannot completely lose their freedom. Every possible statement or perception contains both terms — the self and that which it perceives or states.[23]

22 Yeats was quite happy to call the One "God," and did so quite regularly in his writing. We should not, however, infer from this that Yeats espoused as his own the Christian concept of God, as Virginia Moore does too eagerly in *The Unicorn*. The critical confusion surrounding Yeats's religious beliefs originates in his willingness to accept all metaphors for reality, for in his view each culture has a legitimate, if different, set of references to describe and understand the same truth. He accepted the religious myths and terminology of Christianity as readily as he did those of Druidism and of various Eastern religions.

23 First quoted by V. Moore in *The Unicorn*, pp. 378-80.

In these propositions, Yeats stated clearly that human life is only a gyre or a part of a gyre, and therefore incomplete. The external universe cannot then be created solely by the human mind, but is a joint creation of all spirits perceiving each other (the sum total of reality) in unison. This point has generally been misunderstood by critics of Yeats's thought. Robert Snukal, for example, in his study of Yeats's philosophical poetry, states that "In the 'Seven Propositions,' Yeats argues that reality is a function of the human mind."[24] Using this as a starting point, Snukal goes on to distinguish between the position of Yeats on the nature of the spirit and that of Plato and Plotinus:

According to both Plato and Plotinus, one could escape from the wheel, could achieve a unity with the one, and thus lose personality and escape rebirth. In Yeats's cosmology, however, there is nothing beyond the human mind. The suprasensual world is simply the mind, and this mind cannot be confused with another greater mind.[25]

In fact, as both the philosophical treatises and the plays make abundantly clear, the human spirit is indeed but a fragment of that greater being for Yeats as for Plato and Plotinus. Since separation from the One spells unhappiness, the goal of the spirit (thought it often loses sight of this goal when it becomes immersed in any one life) is to journey through the cycles of birth and rebirth, up the hierarchy of being in order to return to unity of being, a phrase which Yeats used to signify complete unity with the One. The main difference between Yeats and Plato and Plotinus on this point is the importance that Yeats places on the human experience. Though human life is by definition unhappy, it is nevertheless cherished by his protagonists, who are torn between the vague, unsatisfied desires which make them long for an end to separation, and the passions and memories of this life.

The plays chart the bittersweet, conflict-ridden journey of mortals through human lives; this journey can be a physical one such as Forgael's sea voyage in *The Shadowy Waters*, or a psychical one such as Cuchulain undertakes in *The Only Jealousy of Emer*. The Cuchulain cycle as a whole can be understood as a journey from youth to old age, from innocence and foolhardiness to experience and wisdom. Many of Yeats's protagonists are wanderers at heart, and their various journeys have distinctly spiritual overtones – many of these characters echo Paul Ruttledge's sentiment in *Where There is Nothing* that "as I can't leap from cloud to cloud I want to wander from road to road. . . . Did you ever think that the roads are the only things that are endless . . . ? They

24 R. Snukal, *High Talk: The Philosophical Poetry of W. B. Yeats* (Cambridge: Cambridge University Press, 1973), p. 41.
25 Snukal, *High Talk*, p. 29.

are the serpent of eternity" (*VP1* 1081). In alternate terms, they long for voyages and adventures of the type glorified by the Grail legends.

It should come as no surprise that there are deep and significant parallels between the adventures of Yeats's protagonists and those of the knights of the Holy Grail. While *The Green Helmet* is the play most obviously influenced by the Grail myths, it can be argued that *At the Hawk's Well* is a failed quest, depicting a callow, vainglorious hero not yet worthy of seeing the Holy Grail – the similarity between the dry well and the boundless spring which dries up in Lancelot's presence can hardly be accidental.[26] Other echoes of the Grail myths in the plays are found in recurring images of the deer and hound which appear so frequently in *The Shadowy Waters* and its companion piece, *The Wanderings of Oisin* – and whose debt to the Grail stories Yeats himself acknowledged in the notes to that poem (*VE* 806) – and of the magical ships of *The Shadowy Waters* and *At the Hawk's Well*.[27]

These echoes of the Grail myths in the plays are no accident. Yeats was profoundly influenced by the Grail stories at an early age, and the rituals which he planned for his proposed Celtic magical order, and which resemble his plays on many points (they also "describe the history of the soul"), were going to be based explicitly on the legends of the Grail: "There will be many degrees . . . and these will describe the history of the soul through the symbolism of the quest of the Grail and the coming to the castle of the Grail, which is to us the country of the dead and of all wisdom. It will be in the degree of the castle that our knowledge will be taught" (*SB* 202-203). Like the knights of the Holy Grail and like the Wayfarer in the unfinished Celtic rituals, Yeats's protagonists are generally spiritual seekers, embarked on an upward or inward journey in which they struggle to escape the bonds of the mortal condition and to regain a higher spiritual existence. Paul Ruttledge, who abandons a comfortable existence for a life of wandering and hardship, and who becomes first a monk and then a spiritual leader, is the quintessential seeker, and it is not surprising that *Where There is Nothing* is the play which most closely resembles the rituals for Yeats's Celtic Mysteries (*CMK* 196).

26 P. M. Matarasso, ed. and trans., *The Quest of the Holy Grail* (New York: Penguin Books, 1969), p. 172.

27 Like Yeats's plays, the Grail legends are derived from Celtic myth, "where the rudderless ship, to which the hero entrusts himself, transparently denotes the acceptance of life's adventure and its concomitant perils and rewards. The ship, too, offers passage to the Other World, and it is noteworthy that in the *Quest* these craft either ferry the emissaries of heaven or hell, or carry the chosen knights on voyages of spiritual discovery" (Matarasso, ed. and trans., *The Quest of the Holy Grail*, p. 289, n. 25).

But Paul is by no means the only spiritual wanderer in the plays. Forgael in *The Shadowy Waters* is a magician in some versions of the play, identified, like Cuchulain in the Irish legends, with those early magicians, the Druids; both Forgael and Cuchulain strive to become one with the gods while seeking for a knowledge, and a condition, denied to humankind.[28] Whether rebels, saints, poets, or lovers, they are all driven by a vague, nameless desire, a desire which, says the Fomorian god Tethra in *The Shadowy Waters*, was unleashed at creation and cannot be satisfied until the end of creation. They all seek, though through different paths, the same unattainable object. The various journeys of the mortal protagonists in the plays are in fact different manifestations of the journey upon which all spirits embark at creation, and which they pursue through all levels of being, seeking to slake a thirst which can only be quenched by the reunification with the true object of desire at the end of separation, the extinction of creation.

However, this journey is "no orderly descent from level to level, no waterfall but a whirlpool, a gyre," as Yeats wrote of life in *A Vision* (*AV* (B) 40). The journey is a continuous struggle, and the spirit, immersed in this struggle, keeps losing sight of that ultimately spiritual goal. While Yeats's seekers have a better understanding of the purpose of life than do their fellow mortals, they too, like Cuchulain in the middle plays, and like Martin Hearne in *The Unicorn from the Stars*, keep losing sight of it. Here lies one of the significant differences between *Where There is Nothing* and the play which replaced it and which Yeats greatly preferred, *The Unicorn from the Stars*. In the former, the protagonist is a saint-like figure who is too often above the workday fray, while in the latter the protagonist is a flawed mortal who struggles throughout the play to remember his true goal, committing many blunders in the process.

This struggle is fraught with conflict as much as with unsatisfied desires. There is no escape from conflict at any level of creation, since for Yeats creation *means* conflict, through the division of the One into innumerable, separate beings; there will be no resolution of this conflict until the end of time. This conflict is manifested in several ways in the plays, as a conflict among mortals, but also between mortals and

---

28 S. B. Bushrui points out Forgael's role as a magus in *Yeats's Verse Plays: The Revisions 1900-1910* (Oxford: Clarendon Press, 1965), pp. 9-10; Druidic magical rituals, and particularly their propensity for human sacrifice such as the Fomors demand of Forgael, are described by Charles Squire in *Celtic Myth and Legend* (Hollywood, Calif.: Newcastle Publishing, 1975), pp. 36-37. V. Moore quotes from John Rhys, who states that Cuchulain "was educated at the school of which Cathbad a Druid was the master ... who had ... made him a master of inquiry in the arts of the God of Druidism and Magic," in *The Unicorn*, p. 49.

discarnate spirits, and even between discarnate spirits. The most important conflict is perhaps that between the individual and his or her "fate," in the battle between free-will and determinism which is central to Yeats's plays.

It is unquestionable that Yeats accepted the journey of the spirit along the hierarchy of being as literally true. It is for this reason that, though Yeats's understanding of the history of the soul in its largest context has definite parallels to his understanding of the workings of the individual imagination, this study is concentrating on unravelling only the former. Yeats's pronouncements on the history of the soul have too often been understood only as metaphors for the creative processes of the individual (and in particular the subjective, or *antithetical*) mind.[29] Helen Vendler's *Yeats's Vision and the Later Plays*, for example, the first book to make a systematic study of the plays in conjunction with the philosophical treatises, reduces Yeats's philosophical beliefs to a system of poetic images. Yeats's "metaphors for poetry" become in her book metaphors *about* poetry and about the creative process of the poet; her central thesis is that *A Vision* is solely "a series of metaphorical statements about poetry, . . . the poet's vision in a metaphorical disguise."[30] While Vendler's approach is often useful, it is perforce limited, and she runs into problems when she tries to interpret metaphorically statements which Yeats (or his instructors) meant quite literally.

A case in point is Yeats's understanding of unity of being. While he claimed that unity of being in its largest sense, as the final union of all spirits at which all desire and all separation ceases, can only be achieved at the destruction of creation, he also claimed that individual unity of being, the union of the creator with the object of his creation, can be achieved by the subjective (*antithetical*) mortal, particularly at Phase 17 of the Great Wheel. The difference is that the desire for unity of being is only temporarily assuaged at this phase, since the mortal must experience many subsequent phases of the wheel of life, and cannot be completely satisfied until the spirit joins its *true* object of desire, of which all objects in an incarnate state are merely a representation, in the final union, the return to the One. Vendler has some difficulty separating these two concepts, since metaphorically they describe the same process, and is forced into a number of elaborate explanations of Yeats's system:

29 Yeats divided men and women in *A Vision* into two main groups, into those striving towards subjective (*antithetical*) completion, and those striving towards objective (*primary*) completion.

30 Helen H. Vendler, *Yeats's Vision and the Later Plays* (Cambridge, Mass.: Harvard University Press, 1963), p. 30.

In some ways, we can regret that Yeats identified the fusion of thought and image by two different symbols . . . but the seemingly needless duplication was inevitable because he had already split his system in two, into "incarnate life" and "discarnate life," into Faculties and Principles, and therefore he required a symbol of perfection for each half of the system.[31]

These are not equal though separate parts of the system, as Vendler suggests; one fits into the other, because incarnate life is only a section of the larger system, which comprises the whole. The same applies to the Faculties and Principles in Yeats's system: while the faculties do influence incarnate life, the period from birth to death, the Principles influence both incarnate and discarnate life, or the period from birth to birth (*AV* (B) 188). Thus the gyre of the Faculties whirls in one-half of the gyre of the Principles (*AV* (B) 201), just as human life, according to Proposition VII, whirls in "a gyre or part of a gyre, whereas reality is a sphere."[32] Vendler's book acknowledges only part of Yeats's system, concentrating on the human, and in particular the poet's, condition, and thus excluding the totality of the soul's experience, of which human life and human creations, while real, are also merely symbols. In this study I hope to redress that balance.

Yeats wrote to T. S. Moore, "my own belief is that we know nothing . . . but 'spirits and their relations'" (*TSML* 66-67). It is therefore not surprising that "spirits and their relations" constitute a major thematic link between the plays. In the next chapters I will chart the journey and struggle of these spirits in the drama. Chapter 2 begins with the emptiness at the source of creation, then examines Yeats's theories on creation, on the separation of the One into the many, and on the hierarchy of being and the conflict between the various orders of being, with particular reference to their manifestation in the plays. Chapter 3 traces the journey of the spirit from creation, through the cycles of birth and rebirth, as it is documented in the plays through the theme of memory, of forgetting, learning, remembering, and forgetting once again. Chapter 4 studies the plight of the soul in the human condition, and its struggle to assert its will in the face of the forces of determinism which seek to control it. The ultimate conclusion of this struggle must

---

31 Vendler, *Yeats's* Vision, p. 69. Vendler refers to Phase 15 rather than 17 because, even though Yeats clearly states that in Phase 15 "there is still separation from the loved one" (*AV* (B) 136), this phase, being out of body, is a better *symbol* than is Phase 17.

32 Note the similarity to Plotinus's "doctrine of the two logical moments" which, as J. M. Rist explains, states that "in finite Beings . . . there are aspects of finitude and infinitude. The One, in contrast to this, is infinity itself" (*Plotinus: The Road to Reality* [Cambridge: Cambridge University Press, 1967], p. 31).

be the reconciliation of chance and choice; the spirit, being "free and yet fast," will "sink into its own delight at last" (*AV* (B) 304). The circle will thus be complete – by pursuing the struggle through the gyres of incarnate and discarnate lives, of finitude and infinitude, of consciousness and the unconscious, we will inexorably return to the beginning.

2

"Spirits and Their Relations"

And then he laughed to think that what seemed so hard
Should be so simple. . . .
("The Phases of the Moon," *VE* 377)

Yeats had seemingly unorthodox ideas about the origin of the universe (unorthodox for a Christian, certainly), and these ideas dictate the setting of the plays. His plays evolve within the world as we know it, but it is a world defined by its original creation and by its ultimate destruction. These boundaries are almost palpable; many of the characters, particularly in the early plays, recall creation vividly and with great sorrow, and long for an end to their suffering and for the destruction of the world. The world of the drama is also sharply defined by its proximity to, but difference from, innumerable other worlds. Yeats's ontology is as unorthodox as is his cosmology; both must be unravelled if we are to understand what Yeats means by the spirit, and to grasp the role and relation of the dizzying number and variety of spirits who appear in the plays.

For Yeats, the universe emerged out of nothing, out of a boundless darkness which existed before generation and which continues to surround it. This nothingness can also be defined as complete unity, a sphere which is complete and immutable and eternal. At creation a form of energy emanates from the sphere which, being separate from it, begins the process of differentiation by which nothing gives birth to the many, innumerable spirits who are all equal, and each of whom forms an integral and necessary part of the whole. These separate beings are "spirits" in Yeats's terminology, though they will assume many different identities as they proceed through the realms of creation, both as individual spirits of all descriptions and as the external forces of the universe which impinge upon these individual spirits.[1]

---

1 Interestingly enough, this theory of creation closely resembles the view of post-Einsteinian physicists, who now posit that all matter, energy, and light emerged all at

Immediately following creation, these spirits coexist in harmony in that "timeless and spaceless community of Spirits" which Yeats called reality in "The Seven Propositions." However, because it was separated from the original unity and therefore from itself at creation, each of these beings must undertake its journey through creation alone, seeking for the Higher, or whole, Self which it has lost. This journey will take it down through almost endless phases of being, where it acquires more and more layers of individuation which separate it from all other spirits until, as a soul imprisoned in a human body, it attains the most extreme differentiation possible. This is not to denigrate the importance of life. Most of the plays, particularly the later plays, celebrate the importance of this life in the development of the spirit, and stress the passion, pain, and joy of life which the discarnate spirits envy.

When its journey on earth reaches an end, the spirit does not cease to be, but simply evolves upward, gradually shedding its layers of differentiation, until it joins its Higher Self, or all the spirits who form the external universe, in the final union which ends differentiation. This is what Yeats postulated in his notes to *The Resurrection*:

We may come to think that nothing exists but a stream of souls, that all knowledge is biography, and with Plotinus that every soul is unique; that these souls, these eternal archetypes, combine into greater units as days and nights into months, months into years, and at last into the final unit that differs in nothing from that which they were at the beginning: everywhere that antinomy of the One and the Many that Plato thought in his *Parmenides* insoluble, though Blake thought it soluble "at the bottom of the graves."

(*VPl* 935)

Spirits live in harmony for a relatively short time following creation, for in Yeats's metaphysics differentiation leads to division and conflict. For Yeats all life can be defined as conflict; as he explained to Ethel Mannin while discussing *The Death of Cuchulain*, "To me all things are made of the conflict of two states of consciousness, beings or persons, which die each other's life, live each other's death. That is true of life and death themselves" (*L* 918). Every being within creation is striving for an end to separation, for a return to the original unity. This can be achieved only through the struggle with its opposite, since perfection or completion in Yeats's view is not escape from conflict so much as it is a reconciliation of opposing forces; "all the gain of man comes from

once, out of nothing (the Big Bang theory), and then expanded to become the millions of entities in the universe. The universe is still expanding and dividing, according to this theory, but at some future point it must stop expanding, and then the fields of gravity of the various planetary bodies will attract each other gradually (the Big Crush theory), until all join together and extinguish each other, thus returning to nothing.

conflict with the opposite of his being" (*AV* (B) 13). For this reason the spirit is always attracted by its opposite; in the words of Peter, an actor in an early version of *The Player Queen*, "We must always love what we are not: the coward loves courage, the sluggish, energy, the sad, delight, the foolish, wisdom" (*MPQ* 115). Though the reconciliation of opposites is striven for during human incarnations, it is not possible, except at the fleeting moments of ecstasy experienced by lovers, saints, and, in particular, poets, until the spirit passes through its prescribed cycles and returns to the final unity at the end of creation: "We attain it always in the creation or enjoyment of a work of art, but that moment though eternal in the Daimon passes from us because it is not an attainment of our whole being."[2] The struggle of the spirit within creation is therefore constant, heralded by one form of conflict or another, whether between spirits at all levels of existence or within the mind of the individual spirit. Decima understands this when she states, in Drafts 11-12 of *The Player Queen*, "It is only by continual struggle, by continual violence we force the gates of Heaven" (*MPQ* 133).

This, in a nutshell, is Yeats's metaphysics. It will be elaborated, and its unfolding in the various plays documented, in the rest of this chapter.

Beyond Unity: "Where there is Nothing, there is God"

The Old Testament begins with Creation: "In the beginning God created heaven and earth." Yeats begins with the boundless darkness which is the source of creation. This darkness is complete undivided emptiness or fulness, in which all individuation ceases; it is the whole, of which all lives, all souls, all worlds are at once a part and a reflection. It is most fully discussed in *A Vision*, which, being essentially a work of sacred geometry, describes it as a phaseless sphere: "The ultimate reality, because neither one nor many, concord nor discord, is symbolised as a phaseless sphere" (*AV* (B) 193). Yeats's use of the sphere to represent reality is not particularly original. The symbol occurs in much of the occult literature in which Yeats was thoroughly schooled and can be traced to numerous philosophers from Plotinus to Parmenides and Pythagoras, as Yeats himself was well aware. Yeats merely added a few embellishments of his own. He wrote that his system "is founded upon the belief that the ultimate reality, sym-

2 From unpublished notes to *A Vision* quoted by Helen Vendler, *Yeats's Vision and the Later Plays* (Cambridge, Mass.: Harvard University Press, 1963), p. 69.

bolised as the Sphere, falls in human consciousness, as Nicholas of Cusa was the first to demonstrate, into a series of antinomies" (*AV* (B) 187). The antinomies most easily mistaken for the sphere are the Four Principles, the *Celestial Body*, *Spirit*, *Passionate Body*, and *Husk*,[3] which Yeats roughly equated with the Plotinian Triad, the One, the Divine Mind or One-in-Many, and the All-Soul (*AV* (B) 194).[4] Nevertheless, while Plotinus understood reality to be the union of all things in the One, Yeats's ultimate reality is beyond even that unity — "The resolved antinomy appears not in a lofty source [the Plotinian One, or Yeats's *Celestial Body*] but in the whirlpool's motionless centre, or beyond its edge" (*AV* (B) 195).

The symbols which dominate *A Vision* are the gyres and cones which represent the ceaseless, whirling, ever-changing motion of the cycles of life and death rather than the motionless sphere[5] because, in Yeats's words, "My instructors, keeping as far as possible to the phenomenal world, have spent little time upon the sphere, which can be symbolised but cannot be known" (*AV* (B) 193).[6] These gyres and cones are, like the fleeting phantoms of desire of Yeats's early works, "in themselves" merely "pursuit and illusion" (*AV* (B) 73); like the life within time and space which they represent, they only "mirror reality." The sphere, which Yeats equates with eternity, "the final place of rest" (*AV* (B) 69), *is* reality. The sphere encompasses everything; it is the serpent with its tail in its mouth, the beginning and the end and everything in between. Yeats reiterated this in his "The Seven Propositions," where he stated that "The acts and nature of a Spirit during any one life are a section or

3 Cf. "The Completed Symbol" chapter of *A Vision* for a thorough discussion of these four Principles. Yeats defined them as follows: "*Spirit* and *Celestial Body* are mind and its object (the Divine Ideas in their unity), while *Husk* and *Passionate Body*, which correspond to *Will* and *Mask*, are sense (impulse, images; hearing, seeing, etc., images that we associate with ourselves — the ear, the eye, etc.) and the objects of sense. *Husk* is symbolically the human body. The *Principles* through their conflict reveal reality but create nothing" (*AV* (B) 187-88).

4 J. M. Rist's book, *Plotinus: The Road to Reality* (Cambridge: Cambridge University Press, 1967), is particularly helpful in its meticulous discussion of Plotinus's understanding of the One, similar in many respects to Yeats's sphere.

5 Yeats followed Parmenides in affirming that reality is motionless; he states that motion itself is merely illusion (*AV* (B) 211). In this he disagrees with various authorities, including his early mentor, Mme Blavatsky, who taught that "That which is motionless cannot be Divine" (*The Secret Doctrine*, vol. 1 [Los Angeles: The Theosophy Company, 1964; facsimile of the original edition of 1888], p. 2).

6 Mme Blavatsky in *The Secret Doctrine* agrees with Yeats's instructors that there is little to be gained by discussing the sphere, since it is "An Omnipresent, Eternal, Boundless and Immutable PRINCIPLE on which all speculation is impossible, since it transcends the power of human conception and could only be dwarfed by any human expression or similitude" (Blavatsky, *The Secret Doctrine*, vol. 1, p. 14).

abstraction of reality and are unhappy because incomplete. They are a gyre or part of a gyre, whereas reality is a sphere."

The sphere, or "God," is the complete emptiness out of which everything comes; hence Yeats's stipulation (using Blake's phrase) that "God only acts or is in existing beings or men." In the plays, Yeats usually called it "nothing" rather than the sphere, following the explanation which he included in his short story, "Where There is Nothing," in which a priest describes the universe to a small child as a series of nine crystalline spheres beyond which lies nothing, or God (M 184-85).[7] In an essay on George Yeats, R. Ellmann has made much of Yeats's use of the word "nothing" in his later works, and in particular in the later plays. Writes Ellmann:

> In May 1938 he [Yeats] wrote a quatrain for Edith Shackleton Heald in which he offered, as "the explanation of it all," that
> > From nowhere into nowhere nothing's run.
> The same words resound in two of his last plays: the old man in *Purgatory* says at the end, "Twice a murderer and all for nothing," and the last speech of *The Herne's Egg* includes the line, "All that trouble and nothing to show for it...." Yet in another late work, the poem entitled "The Gyres," Yeats insisted that out of "any dark rich nothing" the whole gazebo would be built up once again. He could conceive of nothing as empty and also as pregnant.[8]

Exactly. Ellmann proceeds no further with the argument; he seems convinced that this is an undefined new direction that Yeats was taking in his "speculations about final matters" towards the end of his life. In fact, the "rich, dark nothing" out of which creation has sprung, and the possibility of destroying creation in order to return to it, are images Yeats used repeatedly, almost obsessively, in the early plays and in such poems as "He mourns for the Change that has come upon him and his Beloved, and longs for the End of the World":

> I would that the Boar without bristles had come from the West
> And had rooted the sun and moon and stars out of the sky
> And lay in the darkness, grunting, and turning to his rest.
> > (*VE* 153)

A cancelled variant to the first ritual of Yeats's Celtic Mysteries (written before 1902) is more explicit. There the Wayfarer is admonished to

---

7 J. M. Rist argues that, though Plotinus never actually called the One "nothing," such an attribution is the logical extension of his understanding of the One: "The One then is no particular finite Being. It is, as Plotinus frequently says, 'other than Being.' Since it is not a finite Being, can it be reasonably said that it is 'not-Being beyond Being,' as Porphyry puts it (Sententiae, ch. 26) or even 'Nothing,' the term ventured later by Scotus Erigena? We can doubtless trace the historical sequence which led to Erigena's suggestion..." (Rist, *Plotinus*, p. 29).
8 R. Ellmann, "At the Yeatses," *New York Review of Books*, May 17, 1979, p. 25.

"look into the dragons' eye that you may see that which is beyond joy and sorrow. You see nothing there" (*CMK* 226, no. 85).

In the play *Where There is Nothing* Paul Ruttledge attempts to destroy the order of the created world in order to restore the original chaos and reachieve nothing, or God. Paul longs to escape the world, for he believes that "at death the soul comes into possession of itself, and returns to the joy that made it" (*VP1* 1160). He understands, however, that death of the body does not mean an end to his soul's wandering; he must destroy all of creation in order to find this "joy." At first he exhorts his followers to tear down towns, institutions, and churches, but then he remembers that, because the world is spirit, and imagined by spirits, the destruction must take place within minds and souls: "I was forgetting, we cannot destroy the world with armies, it is inside our minds that it must be destroyed, it must be consumed in a moment inside our minds" (*VP1* 1158). Paul strips himself of all his wordly attachments in order to *become* nothing, and offers the same to his followers. "Every religious teacher before me has offered something to his followers, but I offer them nothing. My sack is quite empty. I will never dip my hand into nature's full sack of illusions; I am tired of that old conjuring bag" (*VP1* 1154-55). Patricia McFate and William Doherty, in their essay on this play, point out the parallel between Paul's conclusions and the conclusion at which the Wise Man arrives at the end of *The Hour-Glass* when he says, "We sink in on God, we find him in becoming nothing – we perish into reality."[9] Yeats offered another variation on this theme to T. S. Moore: "We free ourselves from obsession that we may be nothing. The last kiss is given to the void" (*TSML* 154).

Martin Hearne in *The Unicorn from the Stars*, a reworking, with considerable help from Lady Gregory, of *Where There is Nothing*, reaches a similar conclusion at the end of that play:

We must put out the whole world as I put out this candle [puts out another candle]. We must put out the lights of the stars and the light of the sun and the light of the moon [puts out the rest of the candles], till we have brought everything to nothing once again. I saw in a broken vision, but now all is clear to me. Where there is nothing, where there is nothing – there is God!

(*VP1* 709)

In the same way Lazarus in *Calvary*, who has welcomed death, will not forgive Christ for resurrecting him, for dragging him back to the light and denying him death and the waste spaces "where there is nothing" (*VP1* 783).

---

9 P. E. McFate and W. E. Doherty, "W. B. Yeats's *Where There is Nothing*: Theme and Symbolism," *Irish University Review* 2, no. 2 (1972), p. 153.

The desire to destroy creation in order to return to the darkness which is nothing is expressed by the protagonists of quite a number of Yeats's early plays. In *The Land of Heart's Desire*, Mary longs for the destruction of the world, as she indicates in the following conversation with her husband:

SHAUN:
> Would that the world were mine to give you,
> And not its quiet hearths alone, but even
> All that bewilderment of light and freedom,
> If you would have it.

MARY:
>   I would take the world
> And break it into pieces in my hands
> To see you smile watching it crumble away.

(VP1 193)

In *The Countess Cathleen*, the poet Aleel, at the news of Cathleen's death, curses the world and longs for the same destruction:

> And I who weep
> Call curses on you, Time and Fate and Change,
> And have no excellent hope but the great hour
> When you shall plunge headlong through bottomless space.

(VP1 165)

Forgael, in *The Shadowy Waters*, hopes for a similar destruction, crying, "There is no good hour but the hour when the gods and the stars alike shall perish" (*TPBS* 44). The editors of the manuscript versions of this play offer a concise explanation of Forgael's desire:

> In its essence, Forgael's burden of wisdom is a recognition that the world (... sometimes embracing ... all creation) has no distinct reality, but consists only of appearances emanating from himself; or in the alternative terms that are also offered, all lives – those of plants, beasts, men and gods alike – are merely a flight from the single great spirit.... Freedom from the burden of living through a succession of delusive lives can come only with the extinction of creation and Forgael's *cri de coeur* is for the great hour when all creation will be quenched.

(DrC 7)

Yeats built both an idealist and a realist view of reality into this play – while the world is a subjective delusion on Forgael's part, a "tower made of polished black stones which each reflect his face" (*TPBS* 44), it is the joint creation of other spirits as well, and therefore has an objective reality which he cannot destroy merely by wishing it away.

The desire for the destruction of creation is also expressed by many of the discarnate spirits in the plays. "The alliance of the Fomor [the gods of darkness] with Forgael," write the editors of *Druid Craft*, "has . . . most of its binding power in their common desire for an end to the order of nature" (*DrC* 8); the devils in *The Countess Cathleen* also long for the day when their "master will break up the sun and the moon / And quench the stars in the ancestral night / And overturn the throne (thrones) of God and the angels" (*VP1* 51). It may well be that the gods of darkness have a vested interest in returning to the ancestral darkness, though it is a darkness that, as Yeats wrote in the notes to "The Wind Among the Reeds," "will destroy all the gods as well as the world" (*VE* 809). More interesting is the desire of the gods of Light for this same destruction. In *The Shadowy Waters* as well as in its companion piece *The Wanderings of Oisin*,[10] Aengus, who is the loftiest God among Ireland's legendary gods, the Tuatha de Danaan, also longs for the destruction of creation, and even of his own existence. In *The Wanderings of Oisin*, we are told that

> Aengus dreams, from sun to sun,
> A Druid dream of the end of days
> When the stars are to wane and the world be done.
> (VE 16)

In *The Shadowy Waters*, Dectora describes the Danaans as waiting, "trembling with hope, / The hour when all things shall be folded up" (*TPBS* 14). This is more than a little confusing, since the Danaans, and in particular Aengus himself, are depicted as perfected beings, residing, it is implied, beyond the conflict and tumult of creation.

This confusion is evident from one version of *The Shadowy Waters* to another. In an early manuscript version, the Danaans are clearly the perfected community of spirits which Yeats described in "The Seven Propositions," living in harmony in the "light" which, as we shall see, is more often than not associated with perfection in Yeats's plays:

> o ye bright gods we praise you
> with our love. You are never lonely
> for you live in the light of each
> others faces and your souls are
> like golden drops of joy.
> (DrC 53)

In another version, Forgael describes them in similar terms and implies that they only can pass (and perhaps already have passed) into the nothing beyond creation:

10 Because of its similarities in theme and mood, and because of its greater length, I have found *The Wanderings of Oisin* to be an indispensable gloss on the early plays, and use it as such throughout this study. In it Yeats tried out many ideas which he later reworked in the plays.

None but the children of Danu, the white host
That move in music above the elements
Have gazed in one anothers eyes & passed
Beyond the shadow to the shadowless deep.

(*DrC* 95)

Nevertheless, joyful and serene though they may be, the Danaans in most versions long for their own destruction.

It would appear that this confusion is caused by the clash between Yeats's metaphysics and his dramatic sense. According to the former it is obvious that the Danaans, however joyous and perfected, are still differentiated beings proceeding from creation: while they may be "whatever in that stream [of souls which Yeats defines as the many] changes least, and therefore ... all souls that have found an almost changeless rest" (*AV* (A) 158), they are still within creation, since *nothing* exists outside of it.[11] The word "almost" is very important. The many, no matter how perfected, have still not achieved the complete, changeless, motionless (*AV* (B) 211) rest of the phaseless sphere. Moreover, they are associated with light, while nothing is complete darkness. Forgael seems aware of this when he accuses the Danaans of hiding with their "bewildering lights" (*DrC* 81) the peace of eternity, while Paul Ruttledge specifically associates nothing with darkness, saying that he wants to escape the light of the world for "the dark. Yes, I think that is what I want. The dark, where there is nothing that is anything, and nobody that is anybody; one can be free there, where there is nothing" (*VP1* 1091). Lazarus accuses Christ in *Calvary* of having blinded "with light the solitude / That death has made" (*VP1* 783).

Nevertheless, it is very difficult to dramatize an eternity which is a formless darkness, undifferentiated, unknowable, and indescribable. That Yeats should relent and describe a golden, song-filled paradise is thus understandable. Just as he was to substitute a description of the gyres of life in *A Vision* for that of the sphere, the ultimate "reality," and just as he would describe the "community of spirits" rather than this sphere in "The Seven Propositions," Yeats increasingly substituted a description of the world of the nearly perfected many, usually the kingdom of light of the Danaans or the Faery Kingdom of the

11 This is what R. Snukal does not understand when he states that Yeats, whom he labels a neo-Kantian, never makes clear "whether or not the Absolute [the Ego, or God] has a separate ontological status. It is never clear (for Yeats, as for other neo-Kantians) whether reality is One being, the Absolute, or whether reality is a number of souls, who taken together, are the Absolute" (R. Snukal, *High Talk: The Philosophical Poetry of W. B. Yeats* [Cambridge: Cambridge University Press, 1973], pp. 14-15). Reality, for Yeats, is beyond separation and beyond unity.

Sidhe, for that of the unknowable sphere. Though Yeats wavered back and forth in *The Shadowy Waters*, in the final versions of the play the insistence on a return to "those streams where druids say / Time and the world and all things dwindle out" (*DrC* 285) is dropped, and Forgael moves instead towards a kingdom "of shining women that cast no shadow, having lived / Before the making of the earth" (*VP1* 319). Cathleen ascends to a similar kingdom, replete with shining angels, in *The Countess Cathleen*,[12] while in such plays as *Where There is Nothing* and *The Unicorn from the Stars*, paradise is described as a place of perpetual, joyous conflict!

Creation

> There came a power out of Nothing,
> And it made Beauty and Peace and it
> warred vanity in the darkness, and the
> darkness overcame it.[13]

According to *A Vision*, creation begins at the entrance into consciousness or perception, when the sphere, now the One or the *Celestial Body*, perceives its solitude. Creation, or in alternate terms "the present . . . , the light, the objects of sense" (*AV* (B) 191), has a fairly straightforward purpose: it "exists that it may 'save the *Celestial Body* from solitude'" (*AV* (B) 189).[14] This understanding of creation is reflected in the early works, and in particular in *The Shadowy Waters*. In several manuscript versions of that play, we are told quite specifically that Forgael can find no meaning in life because he knows that the world is merely an

---

12 *The Countess Cathleen* is unique among Yeats's plays in that it was written during a brief period when Yeats, following Maud Gonne's example, was dallying with Catholicism. The images of God, of devils, of eternity in this play are therefore often the conventional Catholic images, though juxtaposed with thivishes and various other Celtic spirits.

13 From a variant to the Cauldron ritual of Yeats's Celtic Mysteries (*CMK* 207). Yeats is referring here not to the darkness beyond creation, but to the darkness of the fallen world, that of the Fomorians, which he sometimes contrasted with the kingdom of light of the nearly perfected Danaans.

14 Creation in *A Vision* is equated with the Third Principle, the *Passionate Body* (*AV* (B) 191). The theme of loneliness has many permutations in Yeats's system. Solitude, being equated with unity of being, is the reward at Phase 15 for the toil of numerous lives (*The Only Jealousy of Emer*, in *VP1* 551, ll. 222-25), but consciousness of this loneliness eventually plunges the spirit back into the remaining incarnate phases:
> And after that the crumbling of the moon:
> The soul remembering its loneliness
> Shudders in many cradles; all is changed.
> ("The Phases of the Moon," in *AV* (B) 62)

illusion, a series of false "others" created as an escape from the loneliness of self. He cries,

> The life of a man is a
> mere days flight from his own
> spirit, the life of gods is
> a flight from their own spirits,
>   . . .   (all)
> things the mountains and the
> seas & beasts & the flowers &
> the fruits with their countless shapes
> & all the races of men have
> taken their shapes & their colours & danced their
> story danced that they might
> for a moment forget now and again forget the
> loneliness of the spirit. It was in
> flight that the world rushed from
> the protection of the mother or [maker] of the
> gods.
>
> (*TPBS* 21)

These "others" can also be understood as a series of mirror images,
gradually more distorted, of the One: "The Soul came out of silence
and out of secrecy, it looks upon itself in many mirrors, that all things
may look upon the soul, for none can look upon it in whom there is no
image of the Soul" (*CMK* 206, n. 22). Once the act of perception
(creation) has taken place, "the present, the light, the objects of sense,"
those refracted images of self which are thus unleashed, immediately
achieve an existence independent of the creator. In *The Shadowy Waters*,
it is Forgael who is the creator/perceiver. As the editors of the early
versions of this play note, several versions argue that the Seabars
(another name for the Fomorian gods, or gods of darkness, which
haunt the play), "are created in Forgael's mind. . . . Once formed, these
creations of Forgael's mind continue to exist. Forgael lies dead upon
the deck, but the Seabars continue to circle around him" (*TPBS* xii,
xiv). Yeats describes in detail Forgael's creation of one such Seabar.
When Forgael falls in love with Dectora, his love becomes a separate,
living entity, a red Seabar; this same Seabar later becomes white when
Forgael's love turns to pity. Explains the white Seabar:

> I was a formless
> phantom floating in the darkness [?]
> until he who lies there [Forgael] loved
> & then I was born but to a crimson
> shape for I too am one of [the?] gods he has fashioned
> with his thought and his desires.
>
> (*TPBS* 24)

Another pre-1896 version completes this argument:

> "but now he was white for
> Forgael was full of pity, and being the spirit of
> his pity he brought the commandments of pity."[15]

Forgael the creator "tire[s] of seeing always the same face," and thinks he may be able to escape from himself through his love for another, separate being, until, in a number of versions, he realizes that even Dectora is a mere reflection of himself:

> away from me. You too.
> You too. Your eyes are but
> my eyes, your voice is but my voice
>
> (*TPBS* 23)

Obviously this argument was more than a little unwieldy, particularly since it proved impossible to subsume entirely in images and symbols. Yeats toyed with other variations of this theme, implying in another version (and thus compounding his problems) that the Seabars were created not by Forgael but by the Danaans, "the gods who had made them in their image" (*DrC* 20). Yeats never completely resolved the problem of how to dramatize his metaphysics in *The Shadowy Waters*; his solution was finally to discard much of the argument, and with it the accompanying symbols, such as the Seabars, in the final version of the play. In later plays he chose to introduce his ideas on creation more subtly, and far more successfully, by marrying them to the Celtic creation myths.[16]

The most succinct account of the Celtic creation myths that I have found, and that which tallies most closely with Yeats's own references to the subject, is found in the chapter "The Celtic Cosmogony" in *The Candle of Vision* by Yeats's friend AE (George Russell). AE, who like Blake was always being visited by the other world, wrote that his book

15 The white Seabar may be a Christ-figure in this play, first of all because he represents pity, just as Christ represents pity in the Wilde story which Yeats was reading at this period, and which later influenced *Calvary*. The white Seabar says that, like all other Seabars, "I too am predatory"; the difference is that "my beak tears my own heart alone" (*TPBS* 24). In this he resembles the pelican in the Grail legends which stabs its own breast to pour its blood over its dead young, and dies as they regain life; this pelican, an abbot tells Bors, signifies Christ (cf. P. M. Matarasso, ed. and trans., *The Quest of the Holy Grail* [New York: Penguin Books, 1969], pp. 181, 186). In the 1896 version of *The Shadowy Waters* which Yeats sent to Beardsley he wrote that "the scene is set immediately before the birth of Christ" (*TPBS* 42).

16 Yeats couched his cosmology in Christian terms in a few of his plays, notably *The Countess Cathleen*, written during a period when he was attracted to Catholicism, and in *Calvary* and *The Resurrection*, but for the most part he preferred to elaborate it, in his plays as in the rituals for his Celtic magical order, in terms of the Celtic cosmology that he spent several years trying to master.

was based on visions of the Celtic deities which he and others experienced. These visions resemble, and may well have included, the "group visions" of Celtic deities which Yeats and some fellow occultists participated in at the turn of the century while devising the rituals for a Celtic magical order. These visions are described in Yeats's papers, along with endless notes on the various Celtic deities and their attributes which Yeats spent several years compiling.[17] Yeats unfortunately abandoned his work on the Celtic pantheon rather abruptly, and his notes on the subject are fragmentary and often confusing. Since Yeats, as their correspondence makes clear, considered AE an authority on matters of Celtic faith, and since he was very familiar with this book, *The Candle of Vision* is a useful starting point for unearthing Yeats's references to creation in the drama.

AE sets out to describe and explain the Celtic creation myths from which the modern Celtic cosmology has descended. In so doing, he claims to discover significant parallels, not only to ancient philosophies (something which must have pleased Yeats) but also to all sacred literatures, from the Bible to the *Upanishads*.[18] He too begins with a complete, undifferentiated unity which he calls "boundless Lir" (*Candle* 153): "We have first of all Lir, an infinite being, neither spirit nor energy nor substance, but rather the spiritual forms of these, in which all the divine powers, raised above themselves, exist in a mystic union or trance" (*Candle* 155). AE agrees with Mme Blavatsky that Lir (in Yeats's terms nothing, or the phaseless sphere) is "devoid of all attributes,"[19] and with Yeats's communicators that little purpose can be served by attempting to describe it: "Of Lir but little may be affirmed, and nothing can be revealed" (*Candle* 153). What is important is that during creation a trinity of powers emanates from Lir and creates the universe. According to AE, this trinity in the Celtic pantheon comprises Manannan, the female figure Dana or Sinan, and Aengus.[20]

17 Cf. in particular two hard-backed notebooks from the late 1880s and early 1890s, National Library of Ireland MS. 13,574, in which Yeats tried to make some sense of the many Celtic gods who were apparently appearing to himself, George Pollexfen and others at this time. Cf. also *CMK* 114-56.
18 AE, *The Candle of Vision* (1918; rpt. Wheaton, Ill.: The Theosophical Publishing House, 1965), p. 163. All subsequent references to this book will be inserted in the text.
19 Blavatsky, *The Secret Doctrine*, vol. 1, p. 14.
20 This Celtic trinity is another variation of the Plotinian triad and, together with Lir, resembles on several points the Four Principles of *A Vision*. AE points out that "Other names might be used in this Celtic cosmogenesis and the Dagda stand for Lir, Boan for Dana, Fintan for Mananna, and others again might be interchangeable with these.... [I]n antiquity races were invaded by others who came with a cosmogony the same in all essentials, but for differences of language and name, as that of the people invaded" (*Candle* 162). He thus explains the bewildering number of interchangeable gods found in the existing fragments of Yeats's Celtic visions and rituals.

Yeats's own research appears to confirm this: among his papers is a list of Celtic gods from Lir to Brigit, in which Lir is numbered as zero and Manannan (sic) as one,[21] while in the existing fragments of his Celtic visions and rituals the references to Manannan (the central figure on the Dais), to Dana ("The Mother of all Things"), and to Aengus ("the Spirit of Life") (*CMK* 154, 174) tally with AE's description of these gods.

Manannan is "the divine imagination" and the "unuttered word" (*Candle* 155): "He is the root of existence from which springs the Sacred Hazel, the symbol of life ramifying everywhere." Manannan conceives "an image of futurity" and focuses it on Dana, "the great Mother and Spirit of Nature, [who] grows thirsty to receive its imprint on her bosom, and to bear again her offspring of stars and starry beings" (*Candle* 154). Now a third impulse or power, "love yet unbreathed" who is Aengus the Young, "awakens as the image of the divine imagination is reflected in the being of the Mother, and then rushes forth . . . to embrace it" (*Candle* 157). Creation has begun: "The Fountain beneath the Hazel is broken. Creation is astir. The Many are proceeding from the One" (*Candle* 157).

It seems that Manannan, Dana, and Aengus are much more important than their role in popular Irish legends – the legends generally referred to by critics to illuminate Yeats's use of these gods – would lead us to believe. AE points out this seeming disparity and explains that the two images of these gods as the creative powers of the universe and as lesser gods of the Sidhe (the Irish faeries) are indeed connected, "for in the mysteries of the Druids all the gods sent bright witnesses of their boundless being, who sat enthroned in the palaces of the Sidhe" (*Candle* 159). Manannan, in AE's description, is unique and set apart from all other gods, for he "alone of all the gods exists in the inner side" (*Candle* 156) of Dana, the Spirit of Nature. The prominence which Yeats gives Manannan in the plays (and in particular in the manuscript versions) is therefore given more basis in tradition.

Manannan's central role during creation is hinted at in *The Wanderings of Oisin*, where he is referred to as the god who built the now crumbling palace in the second island (the island of never-ending battle) "with captive demons sent / Out of the sevenfold seas [the seven streams which issued from the fountain of creation]" (*VE* 38). In early versions of *The Only Jealousy of Emer*, Manannan appears as an impassive, shadowy figure from the Country-Under-Wave, who sits at

21 Dana does not appear, but the second place is given to "the Mor-Reigu" (Reel 29, vol. 4, p. 131, W. B. Yeats Archives, State University of New York at Stony Brook). The Morrigu makes an appearance in *The Death of Cuchulain* as the female daimonic figure who is the representative of destiny.

a chessboard playing with the destinies of lesser beings, both gods and mortals. Fand orders first Cuchulain and then Bricriu to "stand before our King [Manannan] and face the charge / And take the punishment" (*VP1* 561). In his reply, Bricriu, a god himself, acknowledges the power that Manannan has over him:

> I'll stand there first,
> And tell my story first; and Mananan
> Knows that his own harsh sea made my heart cold.
>
> (*VP1* 561)

In *The Green Helmet* Manannan once again personifies fate, particularly since Yeats implies that the Red Man, the antagonist in the play, is in fact Manannan in disguise. As the Red Man, he has tampered unmercifully with the minds and lives of Cuchulain's people in order to test Ireland, and specifically to test, and then reward, the courage of its bravest man, Cuchulain (*VP1* 453).

It is in the manuscript versions of *Deirdre* that Manannan has the largest role, clearly manipulating all of the action, though he is completely replaced in the final versions by omens and premonitions, and by symbols of fate such as the chessboard which a pair of ill-fated lovers play on. In the early versions, Manannan, who in some versions is presented as Deirdre's father, is responsible, first of all, for Deirdre's first meeting with King Conochar [Conchubar in the final versions]. We are told that he brought Deirdre from the Country-Under-Wave and placed her at Conochar's feet in order to start up the commotion that will end with Conochar's destruction:

MUSICIAN:
> And is [Deirdre] the daughter of that god or indeed
> But mortal like us all?

LAVARCAM:
>   None knows for right
> But it may be that Mannan came up
> As many say out of his wealthy stream
> And laying a new born child upon the ground
> Before King Conochar; with a loud cry
> As though he had seen all years that were to come
> Began "this weakling shall grow up a woman
> So coveted by the proud kings of the world
> They shall blow up all to quarrel and in that quarrel
> Your country and all the countries of the west
> Shall go to rack and ruin"; and thereon
> He folded his sea green cloak upon his head
> and vanished.[22]

---

22 Virginia B. Rohan, "The Writing of W. B. Yeats' *Deirdre*: A Study of the Manuscripts" (Ph.D. Dissertation, University of Massachusetts, 1974), pp. 217-18.

Manannan very obviously represents a fate in this play, and it is not just Conchubar's life he is manipulating. In one of the early versions, for example, he casts a spell on the sons of Usnach and on Deirdre's lover, Naoise, rendering them immobile and thus allowing King Conochar to capture and kill them. But it seems that here he is not so much aiding Conochar as helping Naoise and his comrades to fulfill their own destiny and that of Deirdre, for they go to the heavenly kingdom to make joyful preparations for Deirdre to join them:

> NAOISE:
> It is Deirdre's voice! It is coming from a long way off! She is coming over the sea, she is coming by herself in a little boat! She is coming to join us in the happy Plain, the many coloured plain!

> ARDAN:
> Her father the strong son of the sea, who brought us so safely to this place of peace will bring her to us safely.

> NAOISE:
> Yes, let us go, let us make ready the sunny house for Deirdre let us make the pillars of the silver stemmed trees, let us roof it with the blossoming boughs, let us spread silk and needlework.[23]

Manannan is therefore a very important figure for Yeats, and his appearance in the plays, however brief in the final versions, is linked to Yeats's metaphysics and to his understanding of creation and of the relationship of human beings to their destiny (this is discussed further in Chapter 4).

Though Yeats searched through books on Celtic mythology and through his own private sources for information about Dana, he wasn't able to learn very much about her,[24] and in the plays she appears only fleetingly as the mother of the gods of light, the Tuatha de Danaan. Yeats had more success with Aengus. In their joint astral visions, he and his uncle George Pollexfen felt they had made contact with this divinity; Pollexfen, and then Yeats, saw him as a being connecting

23 Rohan, "Yeats's *Deirdre*," pp. 189-90. Manannan's role in the manuscript versions of this play is fascinating, and warrants a more detailed study than is possible here.
24 Dana is referred to in the *Cauldron* ritual for Yeats's Celtic magical order as "the mother of all things etc. Through Danon the soul is withdrawn into the abyss" (*CMK* 174). Yeats's handwritten notes reveal that he was actively seeking information on this goddess: "She was apparently the mother [of] the gods who are called the tribes of the goddess Danu. Her names is identified [?] by Rhys with names meaning 'Darkness' and cognitive ideas. . . . There is little about her in Rhys. She may be a more ancient goddess whose history is now forgotten" (Reel 29, vol. 4, p. 239, W. B. Yeats Archives, State University of New York at Stony Brook).

heaven and earth. Pollexfen, wrote Yeats, "described seeing the lower part of the body of a most radiant figure whose head and shoulders were lost in the clouds" (*CMK* 149). This is how Yeats depicts him in the plays. Aengus is the ruler of the Children of Danu (sic) in such plays as *The Shadowy Waters*, *The Wanderings of Oisin*, *The Countess Cathleen*, and *The King of the Great Clock Tower*, but, as befits a being who connects heaven and earth, even he is subject to the sorrows of creation, and longs for the end of the world.[25] Yeats's description of Aengus tallies quite closely with that of AE in *The Candle of Vision*. For AE "the golden-haired Angus of the Bards" (p. 59) is an "all-pervading divinity who first connects being with non-being." As such he is identified as much with time as with eternity: he is not only divine love or joy (the love child of the marriage of Dana and Manannan), but also the eternal desire which is the reflection of divine love in a fallen world.

> It is Angus the Young an eternal joy becoming love, a love changing into desire, and leading onto earthly passion and forgetfulness of its own divinity. The eternal joy becomes love when it has first merged itself in form and images of a divine beauty dance before it and lure it afar. This is the first manifested world, the Tirnanoge or World of Immortal Youth. The love is changed into desire as it is drawn deeper into nature, and this desire builds up the Mid-World or World of the Waters. And, lastly, as it lays hold of the earthly symbol of its desire it becomes on Earth that passion which is spiritual death.
>
> (*Candle* 157-58)

This last excerpt from *A Candle of Vision* contains, in capsule form, Yeats's own theory of existence within creation: once created, the spirit (represented here by Aengus) quickly forgets its own divinity and journeys down the hierarchy of being in pursuit of false objects of desire. All created beings act out Aengus's own pursuit, according to the "Black Jester" in a discarded Prologue to one of Yeats's plays: "I am going to make you dream about them [the gods]. . . . These two are Aengus and Edaine. They are spirits and whenever I am in love it is not I that am in love but Aengus who is always looking for Edaine through somebody's eyes."[26] Yeats's plays are filled with these objects of desire, many of which take the form of "divine beauty"; immortal

25 Cf. An alternate figure for Aengus in the cosmology elaborated in Yeats's plays is Jesus Christ in *Calvary* and *The Resurrection*. Like Aengus, Christ connects heaven and earth and thus is subject to the laws of mortality. He must go through the cycles of existence, including the torment of purgatory, before he can be freed from the wheel of time and return to eternity.

26 Rohan, "Yeats's *Deirdre*," p. 148. Rohan states that this prologue, which is the prototype for the Old Man's prologue in *The Death of Cuchulain*, was written either for *Deirdre* or for *The Shadowy Waters*.

women, from the Witch Vivien in one of the earliest plays, to Niamh in *Oisin*, to the Hawk Woman in *At the Hawk's Well*, to Fand in *The Only Jealousy of Emer*, all lure mortal men with a promise they cannot fulfill. These false objects of desire are perhaps most conspicuous in *The Shadowy Waters* and *The Wanderings of Oisin*, where "shadows of unappeasable desire," in the form of the hound with one red ear chasing the hornless deer, or the young man chasing the girl with the golden apple in her hand, are central symbols. These shadows appeared at creation, says the Fomorian god Tethra, and constitute one of the two great sorrows he suffered then (the other being his ejection from paradise); they "signal the beginning of frustration and delusion" (editors, *DrC* 20). When Forgael cries, "grant / me an hours / refuge from my own spirit that ever / pursues" (*DrC* 55), Tethra sends him the beautiful Dectora; Forgael immediately realizes that she too is only another such image:

> I am heard.
> Tethra has bid a sign wake in the shield
> The shadows that before the world began
> Made him bow down upon his throne and weep
> And that are in the waters and the winds always
> The shadows of unappeasable desire,
> A boy that follows upon flying feet
> A girl that has an apple in her hand;
> And I am blinded by a foam of dreams.
>
> (*TPBS* 10-11)

This pursuit is ultimately the desire for unity, for the whole from which the individual spirit has been separated by creation. Thus Fand, in an early version of *The Only Jealousy of Emer*, explains her pursuit of Cuchulain by likening herself to the yolk, and he to the white, of an egg that was shattered by his birth:

> As man before he is born into the world
> Is shaped as an egg, a yellow yoke will [=still] is
> About the white of [the] egg, but when he is born
> He's but the white, the yoke remains a dream.
> And both [are] miserable, until they meet at death.[27]

At creation, writes AE, the Sacred Hazel appears, whose branches are the gods,[28] "and as the mystic night trembles into dawn, its leaves and blossoms and its starry fruit [all spirits] burgeon simultaneously

---

27 Steven R. Winnett, "An Edition of the Manuscripts of Two Plays by W. B. Yeats, *The Only Jealousy of Emer* and *Fighting the Waves*" (Ph.D. Dissertation, New College, Oxford, 1978), p. 51.
28 The tree of life of the Kabbalah.

and are shed over the waters of space" (*Candle* 154). The waters of creation at the foot of the Sacred Hazel occur in various guises in quite a number of Yeats's plays. Streams and wells and fountains are referred to often by Yeats, and quite consciously, if his discussion of William Morris's use of similar symbols is any indication:

I do not think that it was accident . . . that made William Morris . . . celebrate the Green Tree and the goddess Habundia, and wells and enchanted waters in so many books. In *The Well at the World's End* green trees and enchanted waters are shown to us as they are understood by old writers, who thought that the generation of all things was through water.

(*EI* 54)

The early versions of Yeats's plays are full of such statements: the fool and Yellow Martin (later Septimus) in *The Player Queen* state specifically that "from water generation comes, but that's a mystery" (*MPQ* 221). In later versions of this and other plays Yeats followed his usual method of perfecting the symbol and discarding the abstraction. Thus wells, fountains, and streams as the source of creation appear in several plays, including *The King's Threshold*, where they are located in the garden of Eden at the foot of "old Adam's crab-tree" (*VP1* 303), and *On Baile's Strand*, where Cuchulain uses this symbol to explain the theory that the spirit weakens as it travels further away from creation:

> If I had fought my father, he'd have killed me,
> As certainly as if I had a son
> And fought with him, I should be deadly to him;
> For the old fiery fountains are far off
> And every day there is less heat o' the blood.
>
> (*VP1* 511)

As often as not, however, these symbols are used not so much in reference to the beginning as to the end of creation, when the seven streams will return to their source, and as such double as symbols for the quest of the seekers in the drama. Forgael is seeking

> some island where the life of the world
> Leaps upward, as if all the streams o' the world
> Had run into one fountain.
>
> (*CP* 497)

At the end of another version he announces that

> our sail has passed
> Even the wandering islands of the gods
> And hears the roar of those streams where druids say
> Time & the world & all things dwindle out.
>
> (*DrC* 284-85)

The poet Seanchan in *The King's Threshold* has various visions of the garden of Eden as he nears death, and finally lies down to await it, "rolled up under the ragged thorns / That are upon the edge of those great waters / Where all things vanish away" (*VP1* 287). And the Wise Man in *The Hour-Glass*, though more reluctant to leave this world, realizes that he too will soon die, because

> The stream of the world has changed its course,
> And with the stream my thoughts have run
> Into some cloudy thunderous spring
> That is its mountain source –
>
> (*VP1* 637)

Another variation of this symbol occurs in *The Unicorn from the Stars*, where the dying Martin longs to climb the mountain of Abiegnos, which in the Rosicrucian lore of the Golden Dawn is the flat-topped mountain at the centre of the world on which is to be found "the great walled garden of Eden."[29] "It is a hard climb," says Martin, "Help me up. I must go on. The Mountain of Abiegnos is very high" (*VP1* 710).

In yet another variation, the well becomes "St. Colman's Well," the "blessed well" of the Druids, where people seeking to find physical health, may instead find spiritual perfection, as in *The Cat and the Moon*, or where they seek immortality, as in *At the Hawk's Well*. It is certain that all these wells and fountains are connected. In the very early play *Time and the Witch Vivien*, for example, the fountain plays two roles, first as the fountain of youth in which Vivien gazes at herself, longing to hold onto life, beauty, and power, and then as the symbol of her death, since it is heard bubbling in the background as she loses the game of chance she has been playing and dies (*VP1* 1279). The well in *At the Hawk's Well* can also be equated with Connla's Well of Celtic creation myths.[30] That Cuchulain, like Forgael, is seeking for perfection outside time in this play rather than for immortality within it is more than plausible, particularly in view of his subsequent attempt to escape the confines of this world which is dramatized in *The Only Jealousy of Emer*.

---

29 V. Moore, *The Unicorn: William Butler Yeats's Search for Reality* (New York: Macmillan, 1954), p. 208. The Adeptus Minor ritual consists largely of questions and answers about the mountain of Abiegnos and the tomb of Christian Rosencreutz.

30 On a letter to her from W. B. Yeats referring to the visions of Connla's Well that they experienced together, the clairvoyante Mrs. Hunter noted that "The magic well of Connla lies at the foot of a mountain ash. Those who gaze therein may, if they can find a guide, be led to the Fount of Perpetual Youth. The ash berries fall into the water and turn them to fire. Connla, the Druid, is the Guardian of the Well" (*L* 293).

The Many

The fountain beneath the Hazel has broken. Creation is astir. The Many are proceeding from the One. An energy or love or eternal desire has gone forth which seeks through a myriad forms of illusion for the infinite being it has left.

(*Candle* 157)

At creation, then, innumerable beings emerge from the original god-head. These beings are all equal; they are also unique, as Yeats stressed repeatedly in his writing. With words almost identical to those whispered to Michael by the angels in *The Speckled Bird* (p. 32), Countess Cathleen affirms that,

> There is no soul,
> But it's unlike all others in the world,
> Nor one but lifts a strangeness to God's love
> Till that's grown infinite, and therefore none
> Whose loss were but less than irremediable
> Although it were the wickedest in the world.

(*VP1* 69-71)

Though all emanate from the One, these spirits forget their divinity as they journey further and further away from creation, becoming lesser and lesser spirits until, finally, they forget their divinity entirely and identify themselves completely with the human body.

Each spirit undertakes its search alone, and progresses at its own pace through the cosmos, so that the cosmos becomes populated by an elaborate hierarchy of beings ranging from the One to humanity. Mme Blavatsky states this theory very succinctly.

The whole Kosmos is guided, controlled, and animated by almost endless series of Hierarchies of sentient Beings, each having a mission to perform.... They vary infinitely in their respective degrees of consciousness and intelligence; and to call them all pure Spirits ... is only to indulge in poetical fancy. For each of these Beings either *was*, or prepares to become, a man, if not in the present, then in a past or coming cycle.[31]

Spirits on various levels can be differentiated by the degree of materiality which they have achieved, for the journey downward to humanity is characterized by a gradual acquisition by the spirit of more and more layers. The spirit acquires the most layers when it becomes human, for it adopts not only the most solid of material forms, but also a personality which blinds it to its divine nature.

The soul clings to its new acquisitions, but it cannot begin the journey upward until it is willing to shed them, to let them go, as Paul

31 Blavatsky, *The Secret Doctrine*, vol. 1, pp. 274-75.

Ruttledge teaches in *Where There is Nothing*. This is what Yeats considered physical death to be, merely a discarding of the form, personality, and memories of this life in preparation for succeeding lives. The magician Dunn/Maclagan in *The Speckled Bird* elaborates on this concept when he says that the physical body grows healthier as the spirit weakens, but grows weaker as the spirit gets stronger – thus the spirit regains much of its strength at death.

> [T]he more we die here, the more we lose what makes up life, the [?] nearer we come to them [disembodied spirits], and . . . when they descend to us and are born, they die in their own world. When one thinks deeply about spiritual things, and brings them near to one by accustoming [?] the mind's eye to see them and mind's ear to hear them, one begins [?] an evocation of the life that prophecies away from this life, not only in the mind, but in the circumstances of life. The circumstances of life are merely thought. . . .
>
> (SB 209)

This world, being but a thought, is not real. In Yeats's philosophy none of the levels of existence at which the spirit finds itself are real – nothing is real save the sphere, or rather *nothing* is real. All levels of being are no more than "myriad forms of illusion," no more real than the objects of desire which the spirit pursues from one existence to another. As Yeats wrote in his *Memoirs*, "A visionary woman once said to me, 'If we could only say to ourselves, with sincerity, "This passing moment is as good as any I shall ever know," we would perish instantly or become united to God.' I suppose because desire would be at an end" (*Memoirs* 210). Nevertheless, most spirits pursue this object first in one form, then another, through one existence, then another, not realizing that what they are seeking is their Higher Self and that it is within them. But more of this later.

Yeats believed, with Swedenborg, that each level of being melds with the next "as though a hand were thrust within a hundred gloves, one glove outside another, and so there is a continual influx from God to man" (*VB* II 316). Such a complex hierarchy of being is virtually impossible to catalogue, particularly since Yeats embraced in his philosophy all the world described by philosophers, visionaries, and magicians, by Thomas More, Swedenborg, Dante, Blake, John Rhys, Irish peasants, all religious texts, and the multifarious magical texts turning up in England at that time. Some of these texts, such as *The Key of Solomon*, which was translated by MacGregor Mathers for use by the Golden Dawn, did in fact attempt to name and describe all the different types of gods, demons, and spirits, and make for highly entertaining reading. As E. M. Butler writes of *The Key of Solomon* in his study, *Ritual Magic*, the author's "highly developed although very confused angelology seems not unlike an attempt to tabulate and describe the ten thousand times ten thousand and thousands of thousands in Revelations."[32] Nevertheless, since many of these levels are represented in Yeats's drama, some attempt must be made to sort them out.

Yeats was drawn to the Ptolemaic cosmology as a metaphor for the universe, and referred to it in a number of plays, notably in *Where There is Nothing*, *The Countess Cathleen* (where the devils claim to be from the ninth, and therefore the highest, sphere of hell), and *The Land of Heart's Desire*. This theory, which divides the cosmos into nine concentric crystalline spheres, beyond which lies nothing, or God, is a useful tool for envisaging Yeats's understanding of the order of being within the cosmos.[33] This world view was adopted by the Western magical tradition, and is described by R. Cavendish in his book, *The Black Arts*: "In the early centuries after Christ the idea spread through the Mediterranean world that the soul comes originally from God and descends through the nine spheres to earth, where it is imprisoned in the human body; the soul longs for reunion with God and can achieve it by climbing back up through the spheres to heaven."[34] Yeats elaborated on this cosmology in his short story "Where There is Nothing":

> "There are nine crystalline spheres, and on the first the Moon is fastened, on the second the planet Mercury, on the third the planet Venus, on the fourth the Sun, on the fifth the planet Mars, on the sixth the planet Jupiter, on the seventh the planet Saturn; these are the wandering stars; and on the eighth are fastened the fixed stars; but the ninth sphere is a sphere of the substance on which the breath of God moved in the beginning."
> "What is beyond that?" said the child.
> "There is nothing beyond that; there is God."
>
> (*M* 184-85)

Nothing, or God, is, in Porphyry's terms, "not-being beyond Being." It is the unknowable phaseless sphere of *A Vision*, and as such is referred to, but does not appear, in the plays. The ninth sphere, "The substance on which the breath of God moved in the beginning," can be equated with the First Principle or the One. Here we can place Dana who, though she is referred to as the mother of the gods, does not appear in the plays, and Manannan who, as the shadowy personification of fate, does. Other representatives of fate in the plays who may be

32 E. M. Butler, *Ritual Magic* (Cambridge: Cambridge University Press, 1949), p. 77.
33 Yeats was also drawn to other metaphors for the universe, among them the Kabbalistic tree of life and the Zodiac, and used them in his work. Yeats's cosmology could therefore be studied in the terms offered by these alternate metaphors with equal success.
34 Richard Cavendish, *The Black Arts* (London: Routledge & Kegan Paul, 1967), pp. 100-101.

placed in the ninth sphere range from the Christian god, the "Light of Lights" in *The Countess Cathleen*, and in *Calvary*, to divine beasts like the Unicorn and the Great Herne (heron). Yeats deliberately linked the latter two figures to Zeus through the legend of Leda and the swan; the Unicorn is seen begetting with the queen in some versions of *The Player Queen* while, in *The Herne's Egg*, the Herne has sexual relations with his priestess, though he uses for this purpose the bodies of seven men, who mistakenly assume that they are tampering with his divine plan by raping the priestess.[35] The play is, in fact, a bad joke played on the men, and particularly on Congal, by fate, the elusive Great Herne.

The eighth sphere is the sphere of the "fixed stars"; "the Fixed Stars being the least changing things are the acts of whatever in that stream [of souls which represent reality for Yeats] changes least, and therefore of all souls that have found an almost changeless rest" (*AV* (A) 158). Here can be placed the perfected community of spirits of which Yeats spoke in his "The Seven Propositions." As we have seen, Yeats often described the paradise for which men long not as an undifferentiated unity or chaos, but as the unity-in-multiplicity (concord) which these spirits have achieved. This community appears in many guises in the drama, but it is usually described with images of light and fire; it is the world of "bewildering lights" which is both the Faery Kingdom in *The Land of Heart's Desire* and the kingdom of Light of the Tuatha de Danaan (*DrC* 81). That Aengus and the Danaans should thus be separated from the rest of creation, the wandering stars, and one step closer to the ninth sphere is particularly appropriate since Aengus is the "divinity who first connects being with non-being" (*Candle* 159). Shortly before his death, the Wise Man in *The Hour-Glass* states that "the sand has run out. . . . For I am going from the country of the seven wandering stars, and am going to the country of the fixed stars" (*VPl* 636).

The wandering stars, the next six spheres (excluding for the moment the first sphere, the physical world), naturally include a great variety of spirits, both good and evil, since for Yeats the levels of spirits become thicker closer to earth.[36] Yeats believed that these spirits, ranging from

35 Helen Vendler misunderstands this point when she writes that in *The Herne's Egg* "The Otherworld is both omnipotent (the Great Herne's curses are deadly) and absurd – [the priestess] Attracta is raped by seven men, but on the morning after serenely asserts that it never happened, that there is no reality but the Great Herne" ("Changing Metaphors for the Otherworld," *Modern Drama* 7 [1964], p. 319).

36 The same spirit will be both good and evil at some point, as Tethra declares, announcing that Forgael "shall be a destroying demon a thousand ages and then take on a shape of light" (*TPBS* 49). In the Shiftings, the third phase between death and life which is described in *A Vision*, "In so far as the man did good without knowing evil, or evil without knowing good, his nature is reversed until that knowledge is obtained" (*AV* (B) 231).

the lowliest shades to the teaching spirits and guides of the universe, are spirits in one or another phase between human incarnations, that is, between death and birth. This is the thesis of the "Soul in Judgment" chapter of *A Vision*, in which Yeats argued that each soul in between human incarnations goes through six different stages in order to shed the memories of one human life and prepare for the next. The first four states constitute Yeats's understanding of purgatory, when spirits purge themselves of their past lives. Here are to be found all manner of ghosts and shades such as those who appear to the medium in *The Words Upon the Window-Pane*, to the Young Man in *The Dreaming of the Bones*, and to the Old Man in *Purgatory*. Once past these four phases, the spirits are freed of their identification with the past. They may remain in the fifth phase for centuries, with no set identity of their own, and take on various roles, as "guardians of wells or temples" (*AV* (B) 233), such as the Hawk Woman in *At the Hawk's Well*, or as teaching or guiding spirits, such as Bricriu becomes for Cuchulain and Emer in *The Only Jealousy of Emer*, and the Morrigu for Cuchulain in *The Death of Cuchulain*; they are also the Irish fairies or the Sidhe, the "shape-changers of legend," as Yeats called them in *A Vision*, who appear in a number of the plays.[37] In the sixth phase, spirits must prepare themselves to re-enter the world and adopt a new personality, and they may try to tamper with their future destiny by manipulating this world, becoming "frustrators." Yeats blamed much of the initial confusion of *A Vision* on just such frustrators, while the magician Maclagan in *The Speckled Bird* scorns séances because of the frustrators' inevitable presence there.[38]

Yeats believed that all these spirits, like the Irish fairies, are plastic and changeable because they lack a solid body such as a human being possesses. These spirits can therefore change form and appearance at will, or take on the appearance expected by the viewer. Yeats stated this explicitly in his *Fairy and Folk Tales of the Irish Peasantry*, when he said, writing of the fairies and lower order of spirits, "behind the visible are chains on chains of conscious beings, who are not of heaven but of earth, who have no inherent form but change according to their

37 This link between the souls of the dead and the fairies is made implicitly in *A Vision*; it is explicit in Evan Wentz's *The Fairy-Faith in Celtic Countries* (London: Oxford University Press, 1911), a book which, as Kathleen Raine has noted, was in large part based on evidence provided by Yeats. Writes Wentz, "Fairyland is a state or condition, realm or place, very much like, if not the same as, that wherein civilized and uncivilized men alike place the souls of the dead, in company with other invisible beings" (quoted from p. 18 by Raine in G. M. Harper, ed., *Yeats and the Occult* [Toronto: Macmillan of Canada, 1975], p. 86.

38 Cf. Chapter 3, "Remembering," for a discussion of these states between lives and their dramatization in the plays.

whim, or the mind that sees them" (*FFT* 2). Elsewhere he wrote that "their world is very different from ours, and they can but appear in forms borrowed from our limited consciousness..." ("Invoking the Irish Fairies," *UP* I 247). The forms which they adopt, particularly once they have shed the "husk" of their former self after the fourth phase, is therefore of little significance, which is why it does not much matter that Cuchulain's immortal love keeps changing form from one play to another. Bricriu appears in the body of Cuchulain in *The Only Jealousy of Emer*, while in *The Player Queen* the ghost of the Queen's father appears in the living body of a beggar who falls asleep whenever the king takes over. The people threaten to execute the beggar for his antics while under the power of the king, but he only laughs, explaining, " 'I laugh because I am breath. You shall be blown away because you are against my daughter. Come on and twist my cloudy neck' " (*MPQ* 235).

Because spirits are so changeable, and also because he accepted everyone's hierarchy of spirits, believing them interchangeable, Yeats often mixed them in his work, for example in *The Countess Cathleen*, where in one long scene Cathleen and Aleel argue as to whether he has been visited by Aengus or by some "angelical being."[39] It does not matter, Yeats would say, since for him, as for the Irish peasantry at large, they are alternate metaphors for the same truth: "Christianity and the old nature faith have lain down side by side in the cottages, and I would proclaim that peace as loudly as I can among the kingdoms of poetry" (*VPl* 1290).

Yeats was doubtless aware of the confusion that innumerable successions of discarnate spirits would cause his audiences and readers, since the published versions of the plays, while still retaining a number of supernatural characters, contain considerably fewer than do the unpublished versions. This is certainly the case with *The Shadowy Waters*, most of whose original cast consisted of the mythological gods of darkness, the Seabars or Fomorians; much of the action develops around their fear and hatred of Forgael, who has become their master, and their even stronger hatred of the gods of light. In the published versions all these gods have been eliminated and replaced by grey birds representing the souls of the dead, who lead Forgael to the end of the world. In the case of this play, however, the elimination of the gods was not entirely his own idea, but was urged upon Yeats by George Moore. Moore describes the role he played in *Ave*, the first volume of his autobiography *Hail and Farewell*. He explains, in his usual mordant fashion, that, in 1899, Yeats

---

39 Cf. the "De Burgh" version of *The Speckled Bird* where the Virgin and the Celtic witch-woman Cailleac Bare become confused in Michael's mind.

had come to Tillyra [home of the dramatist Edward Martyn] from Coole [Lady Gregory's home where Yeats was spending his summers writing] a few days before, and had read us "The Shadowy Waters," a poem that he had been working on for more than seven years, using it as a receptacle or storehouse for all the fancies that had crossed his mind during that time, and these were so numerous that the pirate-ship ranging the Shadowy Waters came to us laden to the gunnel with Fomorians, beaked and unbeaked, spirits of Good and Evil of various repute, and, so far as we could understand the poem, these accompanied a metaphysical pirate of ancient Ireland cruising in the unknown waters of the North Sea in search of some ultimate kingdom. We admitted to Yeats, Edward and I, that no audience would be able to discover the story of the play, and we confessed ourselves among the baffled that would sit bewildered and go out raging against the poet. Our criticism did not appear to surprise Yeats; he seemed to realize that he had knotted and entangled his skein till no remedy short of breaking some of the threads would avail, and he eagerly accepted my proposal to go over to Coole to talk out the poem with him, and to redeem it, if possible, from the Fomorians.[40]

The editors of the manuscript versions of this play posit that Moore may well have done as much harm as good; they argue that by replacing all gods with various types of birds, fate, and other vague symbols Yeats greatly weakened his play (*DrC* 294). Nevertheless Yeats, though more than a little reluctantly, continued to follow the advice of others, and to prune from the published versions the profusion of discarnate spirits encountered in the early versions of his plays. Thus in the later versions of *The Countess Cathleen*, while we still are presented with evil spirits such as Orchil who rises out of hell at Cathleen's death along with her "vapoury multitude / of women alluring devils with soft laughter" (*VP1* 157), we are spared the thivishes and other damned souls who "whisper and fade" at the edge of life, and at great length at the edges of the play. Yeats explained his reasons for the change:

... it seems that my people of the waters and my unhappy dead, in the third act, cannot keep their supernatural essence, but must put on too much of our mortality, in any ordinary theatre. I am told I must abandon a meaning or two and make my merchants carry away the treasure themselves [rather than have the thivishes carry it out].

(*VP1* 1289)

So much for the six wandering stars. The seventh sphere is the physical world, a world not nearly so separate from the others as might be supposed. Many of Yeats's protagonists, like Deirdre, Decima in *The Player Queen*, Paul Ruttledge in *Where There is Nothing*, Andrew in *The Unicorn*, the stroller in *A Full Moon in March*, and Cuchulain,

40 George Moore, *Ave* (New York, 1914), pp. 250-51; quoted in *TPBS* vii-ix.

Forgael, and Oisin, to name but a few, are wanderers, wandering through life because they cannot, in Paul's words, "rise in the darkness under the stars" and "leap from cloud to cloud" (*VP1* 1080). At his death-bed, freed at last, Paul welcomes the Unicorn who will accompany him on his journey up through the spheres, but then, in an interesting twist, balks at going beyond Saturn, the seventh sphere of the wandering stars: "That is right, that is right, take me up in your brazen claws. But no – no – I will not go out beyond Saturn into the dark. Take me down – down to that field under the earth, under the roots of the grave."[41]

That human beings are spirits temporarily residing in a human body is one of the most basic tenets in all the plays. Thus Deirdre says to Naoise before he goes off to fight Conchubar, and probably to his death:

> Bend and kiss me now,
> for it may be the last before our death.
> and when that's over, we'll be different;
> Imperishable things, a cloud or a fire.
>
> (*VP1* 375-76)

Death is transformation, not obliteration. This is the whole point of *The Hour-Glass*, and it is something which many characters in the plays take for granted, though for the Wise Man in that play it is a bitter lesson. Nevertheless, some mortals are closer to being free of their bodies than others, for the hierarchy continues within our own world as well.

While it is clear from the outcome of a number of the plays that people may reach perfection/completion, and shed the mortal condition, at any time, Yeats argued in *A Vision* that most spirits must undergo a minimum of twenty-eight lives on earth, half of them as subjective, or *antithetical*, beings, the other half as objective, or *primary*, beings in order to savour and assimilate all types of experiences possible before they can begin their journey back up through the spheres to the phaseless sphere. The same tale is told in verse in "The Phases of the Moon" and in the opening lyrics to *The Only Jealousy of Emer*, where the musicians marvel at the number of conflict-ridden lives which have gone into molding a woman of beauty:

41 This makes sense when we remember that Yeats depicted Paul as the prophet of a new, *antithetical* age to replace that brought on by the appearance of Christ. Paul therefore resembles Oedipus more than he does Christ. In *A Vision* Yeats reminded Ezra Pound that Oedipus dead, after lying on the ground, "passed with Theseus to the wood's heart until amidst the sound of thunder earth opened, 'riven by love,' and he sank down soul and body into the earth. I would have him balance Christ who, crucified standing up, went into the abstract sky soul and body" (*AV* (B) 27).

How many centuries spent
The sedentary soul
In toils of measurement
Beyond eagle or mole,
Beyond hearing or seeing,
Or Archimedes' guess,
To raise into being
That loveliness?

(*VP1* 531)

In a few of his plays, most obviously in *The Player Queen* and *The Only Jealousy of Emer*, written while he was actively working out his theory of human personality, Yeats seems to have consciously created characters who are at different phases of the lunar wheel described in "The Great Wheel" chapter of *A Vision*, and critics have gone to considerable lengths to identify the phases to which each of the characters belong. Cuchulain, for example, has been identified as a Phase 12 personality, which seems a reasonable assumption since this is the phase of the hero, where a man seeks an image rather than an individual woman (*AV* (B) 129). This is given further support by the fact that Bricriu, who is Cuchulain's daimon, seems to inhabit the phase of the Hunchback, Phase 26, from which the hero derives his mask: in an early version Fand says that Bricriu has "dropped / From a last leprous crescent of the moon." According to F. A. C. Wilson, Eithne Inguba, Cuchulain's young mistress, fits into Phase 14, the phase of many beautiful women. Again this classification seems appropriate; Phase 14 is also the phase of human beings who, though they are languorous and indifferent in appearance, are never at peace with themselves. This would explain Eithne's apparent ineffectuality and timidity, for Yeats states in *A Vision* that "she will wander much alone as though she consciously meditated her masterpiece that shall be at the full moon, yet unseen by human eyes, and when she returns to her house she will look upon her household with timid eyes" (*AV* (B) 132).

Nevertheless, it seems to me that this kind of classification is often rather arbitrary, and can lead to a misreading of the text. For example, using Robartes's comment in "The Phases of the Moon" that "honest wives" are among those found in the *primary* phases, F. A. C. Wilson assigns Emer to Phase 22, and transforms her into a drudge of a wife who is as pious as she is dutiful, and of inferior birth.[42] None of these attributes are based on the text, if only because Yeats wasted little time in describing Emer. Nor are they derived from the legends on which the play is based, for there Emer emerges as a decidedly *antithetical*

42 F. A. C. Wilson, *Yeats's Iconography* (London: Methuen, 1960), pp. 111-12.

character, a king's daughter who is beautiful, courageous, and wise, and Cuchulain's intellectual equal. It would seem to me far more appropriate to place Emer in a phase closer to Cuchulain's since she is the heroine of the play on the dramatic if not on the symbolic level. Surprisingly enough, more recent critics who have argued that Emer is the heroine of the play have made little attempt either to refute Wilson's classification, tacitly accepted even by Vendler, or to place her in another phase.

More serious has been the misreading of *The Only Jealousy of Emer* based on the assumption that the goddess Fand is a perfected inhabitant of Phase 15, the discarnate phase of full subjectivity. Certainly the play seems to give ample evidence that Fand belongs to this phase. Thus Cuchulain, who recognizes that Fand is as unlike all the mortal women he has known as the full moon is unlike its crescent forms, and who seems well versed in the phasal system, identifies her with the pure *antithetical* phase which is symbolized by the full moon:

> Who is it stands before me there
> Shedding such light from limb and hair
> As when the moon, complete at last
> With every labouring crescent past,
> And lonely with extreme delight,
> Flings out upon the fifteenth night?
>
> (*VP1* 551)

Most critics of this play have accepted Cuchulain's assessment, and concur in making Fand the perfected inhabitant of this phase. B. Rajan, for example, while he has difficulty "accepting the Woman of the Sidhe, who, in *At the Hawk's Well*, was the means of Cuchulain's defeat, as transformed into the means of his potential salvation,"[43] feels that he has no choice but to accept that she embodies the complete perfection of Phase 15. Yet Fand's reply to Cuchulain indicates that she has not yet achieved completion: "Because I long I am not complete." Fand later states that though she is closer to completion – that is, perfection – than her mortal sisters, she still "Lacks it . . . by an hour or so" (*VP1* 553) and needs Cuchulain's kiss to make her whole. She comes, therefore, *not* to deliver Cuchulain from the wheel of time, but to deliver herself; the most she can offer him in exchange is "oblivion." Her attempts are frustrated by Bricriu and by Emer, and she never really achieves the subjective completion of Phase 15. In the light of this, it seems to me wiser to use Yeats's "Great Wheel" as a general rather than a specific guide for the study of the mortal characters in the drama.

43 Balachandra Rajan, *W. B. Yeats: A Critical Introduction* (London: Hutchinson University Library, 1965), p. 99.

The characters who appear most frequently in Yeats's drama, Cuchulain and the fool, are at opposite ends of the wheel, the former nearing total subjectivity, the latter total objectivity. The fool is the closest of all mortals to discarnate beings (closer than even the saint), for he inhabits the last incarnate phase of the lunar wheel, Phase 28; in *A Vision* Yeats said of him: "He is but a straw blown by the wind, with no mind but the wind and no act but a nameless drifting and turning, and is sometimes called 'The Child of God.' At his . . . best he would know all wisdom if he could know anything" (*AV* (B) 182). Here Yeats is once again borrowing from the tradition of his magical studies. The Kabbalarian Tree of Life, one of the central symbols studied in the order of the Golden Dawn, is made up of twenty-two paths linking the Sephiroth, or spheres, from Malkus (earth) to Kether (not-being beyond Being). The last path before the attainment of the godhead or Kether is the path of the fool.

This is the role which the fool plays in the drama. In *The Hour-Glass*, the fool is the only one who knows the truth, but he won't (or can't) speak it. In early drafts of *The Player Queen* the fool Mad Michael does speak, but in such a rambling fashion that no one understands him. The fool sees and understands the world which borders on this one as clearly as he does the physical world, and talks about both interchangeably; in this he resembles other visionaries in the plays, such as the witches in *On Baile's Strand*, the musicians in the dance plays, and the attendants in *A Full Moon in March*, who seem to know everything that will affect the protagonists in the plays, but are unable to change the outcome. They are in a sense the touchstones of reality in the plays. On one level, at least, Christ in *Calvary* and *The Resurrection* plays the same role. He is the saviour, the embodiment of hope, but is also a victim because, though he understands the truth and straddles this plane and the next, he cannot really influence either.

One final knot in Yeats's hierarchy of being remains to be untied before we proceed to study the interaction of the various planes of being in the drama. Since "nothing exists but a stream of souls, [and] . . . all knowledge is biography" (*VPl* 935), it follows that, for Yeats as for Eastern mystics, everything around us, even seemingly inanimate matter, is imbued with a soul and is a part of the hierarchy through which all souls descend and ascend. Yeats refers to this possibility in his poem, "He thinks of his Past Greatness when a Part of the Constellations of Heaven," in which a Forgael-like character states that, having been "a hazel tree . . . hung [with] / The Pilot Star and the Crooked Plough / . . . in times out of mind," he later became "a rush that horses tread" before becoming a man (*VE* 177). Though Yeats omitted the possibility entirely from his discussion of the soul's multiple phases of being in *A Vision*, this theme is dramatized most explicitly in *The Herne's Egg*, where he played with the belief that, if a man commits a lowly deed, he may be reincarnated as a beast; Congal in this play will be reincarnated as an ass. Obviously Yeats was influenced in this by Shri Purohit Swami, with whom he was spending the winter of 1937 during which he wrote the play, and by his rediscovery in the last two years of his life of *The Upanishads* (which he helped the Swami to translate) and of Eastern thought generally, a rediscovery he made much of in his letters to AE.

Yeats quite willingly integrated this philosophy into his own metaphysics, just as he did so many other religious systems throughout his life. They are all metaphors for a truth we cannot comprehend; little more can be said. It is best to bear in mind Yeats's remorse, expressed in his journal, after he had argued the truth of reincarnation too forcefully to Maud Gonne: "I remember a pang of conscience. Ought I not to say, 'The whole doctrine of the reincarnation of the soul is hypothetical. It is the most plausible of the explanations of the world, but can we say more than that?' or some like sentence?" (*Memoirs* 48).

Conflict

Spirits on all levels of existence interact in Yeats's plays, and this interaction manifests itself in various forms of conflict. The strife among immortals is less intense than that between mortals and immortals, since, as Yeats wrote in a paraphrase of Swedenborg, spirits are not "divided from spirits[s] as men are from each other, for they share each other's thoughts and life . . ." (*VB* I 316). Thus the conflict of the perfected community of spirits is more like a dance between opposites, a dance which cannot cease until they are joined in the fulness beyond division. In the eyes of several envious mortals in the plays, this divine conflict is a joyous, never-ending battle for which they long. In *On Baile's Strand*, Cuchulain in disgust compares the warfare between immortals to the petty squabbles of mortality:

> though they love to blow a smoking coal
> Till it's all flame, the wars they blow aflame
> Are full of glory, and heart-uplifting pride,
> and not like this.
>
> (*VP1* 522)

Martin Hearne, in *The Unicorn from the Stars*, has a vision in which he claims to visit "Paradise," and describes it thus: "I have seen the shining people. They were all doing one thing or another, but not one of them was at work. All that they did was but the overflowing of their idleness, and their days were a dance bred of the secret frenzy of their hearts, or a battle where the sword made a sound that was like laughter" (*VP1* 688). This is the battle of which Paul Ruttledge speaks when he cries that he wants, "not the fighting of men in red coats, that formal, soon-finished fighting, but the endless battle, the endless battle" (*VP1* 1097).

The battle between mortals and immortals is more bitter, and much more dramatic, since they are opposites in every sense, and "die each other's life, live each other's death." The two worlds, the one visible, the other invisible, are present in most of the plays, and such characters as the fools and the musicians are very much at home in both of them. Their opposition is underscored by a passage purportedly written by a beggar on the walls of Babylon, and quoted by the Wise Man in *The Hour-Glass*: " 'There are two living countries, the one visible and the one invisible; and when it is winter with us it is summer in that country, and when the November winds are up among us it is lambing-time there' " (*VP1* 578). Many of Yeats's plays are actually set on the border between these two worlds, and the encounters between incarnate and discarnate figures take place on these borders.[44]

One such border, perhaps Yeats's favourite, is a wind-swept shore separating this world from the sea, and is the setting of quite a number of plays, such as *The Golden Helmet*, *On Baile's Strand*, and *The Only Jealousy of Emer*. This setting is an integral part of the symbolic structure of these plays, a structure which Yeats was obviously tightening in *The Wanderings of Oisin* when he changed the meeting-place of Oisin and the goddess Niamh from a "vale" to "the dove grey edge of the sea" (*VE* 2). The sea in Yeats's word has a wide range of meaning, and has thus acquired, in B. Bjersby's words, "a symbolic life as changeable as the sea itself."[45] In the drama, however, the sea is a consistent symbol: it is both "Henry More's *Anima Mundi*, Wordsworth's 'immortal sea which brought us hither' " (*M* 346) and the home of discarnate spirits who are inimical to human beings; as such it represents the world between lives. The sea is the home of the sea-gods such as the Fomor in *The Shadowy Waters*, the Red Man and Manannan in *The Golden Helmet* and *Deirdre*, and Fand and Bricriu in *The Only Jealousy*, all of whom are in perpetual conflict with humanity. Many mortal protagonists would agree with Conall in *The Green Helmet* that

44 Cf. Patricia Merivale, " 'Ultima Thule': Ghosts and Borderlines in Yeats and Rilke," *Comparative Literature* 30, no. 3 (Summer 1978), pp. 249-68.

45 Birjit Bjersby, *The Interpretation of the Cuchulain Legend in the Work of W. B. Yeats* (Upsala: A.-B. Lundequistska Bokhandeln, 1950), p. 98.

>   we have nothing to fear that has not come up from the tide;
>   The rocks and the bushes cover whoever made that noise,
>   But the land will do us no harm.
>
>   (*VP1* 422-23)

That *The Shadowy Waters* is set on the sea itself is significant in this context. Forgael's voyage has already taken him far from human life; the sea links him with the Fomor and separates him from his human companions, and it is obvious that despite Aibric's urging his fate is sealed; he can no longer return to mortality.[46]

The sea most explicitly represents the world between lives in *The Only Jealousy of Emer*. The notes to the play posit that the sea is the "womb" of life which has rejected mortals, and to which they strive to return as they wander through human existence, bewildered and alone. The play opens as a solitary sea-bird is cast out of the sea at daybreak onto the shore; the storm-battered bird's plight resembles "the loneliness of the first crab or crayfish that climbed ashore and turned lizard" (*VP1* 571). The opening lyrics concentrate on the tremendous difference between the sea and the land, and especially on the shock of the bird as it is thrown from one to the other. The bird's helplessness is reminiscent of Cuchulain's in the face of his destiny at the end of the preceding play, *On Baile's Strand*, when he battles vainly but furiously with the sea for three days before falling into a trance.

Other specific borders in the plays include Connla's Well, which as the well of immortality separates the mortal realm from the immortal one, and is the meeting-place of Cuchulain and the Hawk Woman in *At the Hawk's Well*, and of the lame and blind men with the Holy Man in *The Cat and the Moon*; the "malevolent woods" of *The Countess Cathleen*, *Deirdre*, and *The Land of Heart's Desire*, in which strange and evil beings wander in the fading light of day; the ruined ancestral home in *Purgatory*, Jonathan Swift's home in *Words Upon the Window-Pane*, and the ruined Abbey of Corcomroe in *The Dreaming of the Bones*, where the living meet the ghosts of the dead; and the mountain-top in *The Herne's Egg*, where Congal is finally done in by the Great Herne. In *The Death of Cuchulain*, the setting is not specified at the beginning of the play, but we are told that "The scene is set," presumably for his death; Cuchulain chides Eithne as she mentions coming dangers, saying:

---

46 I disagree very strongly with S. B. Bushrui's assumption that the sea in this play signifies "the material world" (*Yeats's Verse Plays: The Revisions 1900-1910* [Oxford: Clarendon Press, 1965], p. 9). Its setting on the sea is in keeping with Yeats's understanding of the play as a dream vision, when he writes that "The whole picture as it were moves together – sky and sea and cloud are as it were actors.... It is deliberately without human characters" (*L* 425).

Spoken too loudly and too near the door;
Speak low if you would speak about my death,
Or not in that strange voice exulting in it.
Who knows what ears listen behind the door?

(*VP1* 1055)

Cuchulain in this play seems to be drifting in and out of a trance or dream state; these dream states constitute yet another border in the plays, which have a psychical as much as a physical reality. Thus Forgael is in a dream state much of the time, as is Michael in *The Unicorn from the Stars*. In other plays no setting is given, but the weary itinerant musicians, who are all-seeing, all-knowing, and yet helpless to control the action, are clearly travellers along the border, belonging to neither world but commenting on both.

The conflict between mortals and immortals that occurs at these borders can take the form of good against evil, as in *The Countess Cathleen* and in such simple allegories as *The Hour-Glass* and *The Cat and the Moon*; evil in Yeats's terms is nothing more than "the strain one upon another of opposites" (*M* 357). In *The Shadowy Waters*, the Fomorians plot to kill Forgael because they resent his mastery, while in *The Herne's Egg* the great Herne himself, that personification of "God" or fate, easily crushes those who oppose him. In most plays, however, the conflict is between equals, opposites who are drawn to each other out of some unfulfilled need. The ensuing strife may take the form of a war between the sexes, with the spiritual being assuming the role of the beloved. At other times the conflict is between a human being and his or her true opposite, that other self, either guardian angel or daimon, which exists outside the confines of time and space.

Helen Vendler asserts that "the Otherworld [is] seen in the early plays chiefly in relation to sexual love."[47] Actually, this is true to some extent of most of the plays, because the vague, unspecified desire which is the desire for unity of being takes its first and most obvious form as the desire for union with one's sexual opposite. Immortal women seek out the love of mortal men in such early plays as *Time and the Witch Vivien* and *The Island of Statues*, but already Yeats was wary of the seduction of the other world. In these plays, as in the later *The Wanderings of Oisin*, *At the Hawk's Well*, and *The Only Jealousy of Emer*, immortal women are shown to be as dangerous as they are attractive.

The Wanderings of Oisin describes Niamh, a beautiful goddess from a land "knowing nor tumult nor hate nor strife" (*VE* 9), who falls in love with the mortal Oisin because of the tales she has heard of his exploits in battle. With the best of intentions, she persuades him to leave

47 Vendler, "Changing Metaphors," p. 311.

behind this world of pain and strife for her world. The voyage has disastrous results for both Niamh and Oisin, though, as Yeats later explained in "The Circus Animal's Desertion," "What cared I that set him on to ride, / I, starved for the bosom of his faery bride?" (*VE* 629). The islands to which Niamh leads him are merely worlds of "Vain gaiety, vain battle, vain repose" (*VE* 629), and when Oisin finally shakes her influence and returns to Ireland, breaking her heart in the process, Ireland is as alien to him as were the enchanted islands. Cuchulain's meeting with a goddess in *At the Hawk's Well* proves no more rewarding. Seduced by the dance of the Hawk Woman, Cuchulain forgets to watch the well of immortality and misses the stream of water that gushes from it. The goddess is "the guardian of the well" – as the guardian of the threshold to another world, she refuses passage to those who, like the young, cocky Cuchulain, have not proven themselves to be worthy. Fand's motives for seducing Cuchulain in *The Only Jealousy of Emer* are rather more selfish. Although she represents on the symbolic level the perfection of beauty not possible in this world, Fand is on the dramatic level an incomplete being who needs Cuchulain in order to complete herself, and thus free herself from the lunar wheel. Her seduction of Cuchulain quickly turns into a battle of wills when she discovers that Cuchulain, for his own reasons, is planning to reject her.

It must be emphasized that mortal men desire this union with immortal women just as strongly. However, in Yeats's world view, the hound with the red ear cannot catch up to the white deer until the end of all things, when perfect union will be possible. It follows that once the object of desire has been attained within creation, it is no longer the true object of desire. This is stated explicitly in the sword ritual of Yeats's Celtic mysteries, in which the initiator speaks "of the wanderings of the mind, its search and its longing, never satisfied by the material for more than a moment, for once made concrete the object becomes no longer of the ideal" (*CMK* 182). The seeker must now abandon the false love and seek, once again, for its true love, its opposite or other self outside of time.[48] Yeats made this particularly clear in *The Only Jealousy of Emer* where, in the notes to the play, he explained why the middle-aged Cuchulain is quite right to reject Fand: "Young, we discover an opposite through our love; old, we discover

---

48 Note the resemblance to Shelley's *Athanase*, of which Yeats wrote, "We know too that had *Prince Athanse* been finished it would have described the finding of Pandemos, the [Morning] Star's lower genius, and the growing weary of her, and the coming of its true genius Urania at the coming of death, as the day finds the Star at evening" (*EI* 88).

our love through an opposite neither hate nor despair can destroy, because it is another self, a self that we have fled in vain" (*VP1* 571). Now that Fand's love, which Cuchulain has longed for all his life, is within easy reach, he must turn from it and seek his true opposite, who is in this play the deformed Bricriu. Yeats described this process in a late letter to Ethel Mannin, where he elaborated on his understanding of the relationship of the "sensuous image," or object of desire, to life:

In my own philosophy the sensuous image is changed from time to time at predestined moments called *Initiationary Moments*.... One sensuous image leads to another because they are never analyzed. At *The Critical Moment* they are dissolved by analysis and we enter by free will pure unified experience. When all the sensuous images are dissolved we meet true death.

(*L* 917)

It can be argued that Cuchulain's rejection of Fand in this play dramatizes one such *Initiationary Moment*. That Bricriu is Cuchulain's true opposite, his other self or daimon, is made dramatically obvious in the play, since Bricriu assumes the comatose body of Cuchulain.

The daimon, as Yeats wrote in "Per Amica Silentia Lunae," which he finished just before he began *The Only Jealousy of Emer*, must lead "his victim to whatever among works not impossible is the most difficult" (*M* 361). The daimon is not wholly benevolent, as Yeats hastened to add in "Per Amica"; it also needs completion, which is why it seeks out its mortal opposite: "The Daimon comes not as like to like but seeking its own opposite, for man and Daimon feed the hunger in one another's hearts" (*M* 335). In *A Vision* he was more explicit: "We must . . . avoid attributing to them [the teaching spirits or daimons] the pure benevolence our exhausted Platonism and Christianity attribute to an angelical being" (*AV* (B) 230). It is thus fitting that Bricriu, who acts as the daimon of both Cuchulain and Emer in *The Only Jealousy*, should be the god of discord of Irish mythology,[49] and destroys both Cuchulain's chance to escape with Fand and Emer's hope of recovering Cuchulain's love. But for all this the daimon is also a guiding spirit, a guardian angel. This is in keeping with the magical tradition espoused by the Golden Dawn, which taught that union with his or her guardian angel is the first and most important of the magician's goals. Writes Israel Regardie:

There is, in reality, one perfect ritual in Magic; one goal which takes precedence over all others: the invocation of the Holy Guardian Angel, union with whom

---

49 Virginia Moore paraphrases Arbois de Jubainville on the subject: "the Celtic evil gods are not absolutely perverse; they combine cruelty with paternity – 'one of the strangest and most interesting aspects of the Celtic religion' "(*The Unicorn: William Butler Yeats's Search for Reality* [New York: Macmillan, 1954], p. 55).

should even precede the invocations of the Gods or the Universal Essences. . . . The soul seeks first and delivers its life into the governance of its Daimon, under whose guidance the Gods themselves may be supplicated.[50]

The key to understanding the role of the daimon in the drama is to discover the choices which it is presenting to its mortal opposite in the play, the "hardest work" which it has chosen; it does not matter whether it is motivated by benevolence or by malice. "When I think of life as a struggle with the Daimon who would ever set us to the hardest work among those not impossible, I understand why there is a deep enmity between a man and his destiny, and why a man loves nothing but his destiny" (M 336).

A case in point is *The Death of Cuchulain*. In this play Yeats's immortal goddess appears as the Morrigu; though she is still in love with Cuchulain, she has now taken on the role of his daimon to guide him as he approaches death. That the beloved may become the daimon is given precedence in "Per Amica Silentia Lunae," where Yeats wrote: "My imagination runs from Daimon to sweetheart, and I divine an analogy that evades the intellect . . . it may be 'sexual love,' which is 'founded upon spiritual hate,' is an image of the warfare of man and Daimon; and I even wonder if there may not be some secret communion, some whispering in the dark between Daimon and sweetheart" (M 336). In the 1925 edition of *A Vision* Yeats even claimed, though he later changed his mind, that the daimon is always of the opposite sex, and that therefore the relation of mortal to daimon "may create a passion like that of sexual love" (AV (A) 27). If the Morrigu in this play is understood to be Cuchulain's daimon, and if it is further understood that the daimon can be motivated equally by benevolence and malice, much of the confusion created by her role in the play is easily cleared up.

An essay by Philip Marcus, "Myth and Meaning in *The Death of Cuchulain*," documents the incredible confusion that has ensued from critics' attempts to untangle the Morrigu's motives in the play. But while Marcus argues that the Morrigu is in fact Cuchulain's daimon, he nevertheless falls into the same trap as have the critics to whose interpretations he takes exception. Studying the role of the Morrigu in the play, he first sifts through all the interpretations which claim that she is evil, since she engineers Cuchulain's death. Marcus, citing the authority of the Celticist W. M. Hennessy, argues conclusively that she is in fact "benevolent and protective" towards Cuchulain, and is even

---

50 Israel Regardie, *The Tree of Life: A Study of Magic* (New York: Samuel Weiser, 1969), p. 180.

"'Apparently his tutelary goddess.'"[51] What Marcus does not understand is that the Morrigu can be both benevolent and antagonistic at the same time; she, as Cuchulain's opposite, must lead him to the most difficult of choices. Because he understands her to be friendly towards Cuchulain, Marcus takes this to mean that she must try to dissuade him, however unsuccessfully, from meeting his death. He ends: "Ultimately, however, Cuchulain is not prevented from fighting and dying; and the only thing the Morrigu can do is arrange a dance in which Emer rages against the heads of her husband's slayers."[52]

In fact, the Morrigu knows that for Cuchulain, now an old man, death is timely and fitting. Cuchulain also seems prepared for it, saying at the beginning of the play, though he knows that there is virtually no chance of winning the battle,

> I am for the fight,
> I and my handful are set upon the fight;
> We have faced great odds before, a straw decided.
> (*VPl* 1054)

Once Cuchulain has been led to and has accepted his fate, the Morrigu arranges the dance, not because it is the only thing in her power to do, but because it is the fitting thing to do. Cuchulain has not thwarted the Morrigu's designs, as Marcus argues, nor has he been thwarted by her; she guides him to his death, for which he prepares himself by laying to rest all the ghosts of his life as they appear before him, and he goes off to join the spirits on a higher plane of existence who are described in the companion poem, "Cuchulain Comforted."[53] Once we accept that the relationship between human being and daimon must by definition be characterized by strife, by constant struggle, the variations on this theme in the plays become more readily understandable.

Such is the relation of mortals and immortals; it follows that the conflict within creation is most intense in the physical world, since mortals are the beings most differentiated, and therefore most separated from each other. The conflict of mortals takes its most exaggerated form in *The Player Queen*, the play which Yeats was writing at the same time as he devised his theory of the mask. In one version or another, every character is pitted against another diametrically opposed to itself – Septimus against another actor, Peter, in some versions, against the Prime Minister in others; Decima against Septimus

51 P. Marcus, "Myth and Meaning in *The Death of Cuchulain,*" *Irish University Review* 2, no. 2 (1972), p. 135.

52 Marcus, "Myth and Meaning," p. 139.

53 Cf. Chapter 3, "Acquiring Memories," for a more detailed discussion of this poem in relation to *The Death of Cuchulain*.

on one level, against the real queen on another; the queen against her heroine, the martyr St. Octema, and so on. These opposites must struggle continually; as Septimus says of his relationship with Decima, "there is between her and me a struggle, a trial which of the two is master . . ." (*MPQ*, drafts 8-10, 81). Many of these pairs are on opposite sides of the lunar wheel. In other plays, such as *On Baile's Strand* and *The Unicorn from the Stars*, the protagonists are subjective, intuitive men who are pitted against objective, rational men such as King Conchubar and Thomas, who also represent the repressive forces of the objective era in which the protagonists are living.

The most common form of conflict among mortals, as is to be expected, is sexual love, of which Cuchulain says,

> I think that all deep passion is but a kiss
> In the mid battle, and a difficult peace
> 'Twixt oil and water, candles and dark night,
> Hill-side and hollow, the hot-footed sun,
> And the cold sliding slippery-footed moon,
> A brief forgiveness between opposites
> That have been hatreds for three times the age
> Of his (this) long 'stablished ground.
>
> (*VP1* 478)

In draft sixteen of *The Player Queen*, Decima explains why true love must inevitably result in conflict. She argues that the quarrels between lovers stem from the realization that, no matter how close they become, they must always remain separate beings.

> When he and I have quarreled
> I dread the very mouse that squeaks under the floor
> Yet cannot keep from quarreling because
> As I would have my soul and his soul one
> There is no differing thought too slight to seem
> As it were a wedge thrust down into the soul.
>
> (*MPQ* 212)

Septimus shares Decima's feelings. Although she treats him decidedly badly, and Nona, who also loves him, treats him extremely well, he chooses Decima over Nona — what matters is not that love bring tranquillity, but that it kindle a fire between the lovers (*MPQ* 213). Thus an old woman has little sympathy for Septimus when she hears that Decima has broken his heart, for she says,

> What is that heartbreak but the fiery nest
> (The phoenix nest-life is but born of life)
> Where life, the holy phoenix, comes from life?
>
> (*MPQ*, draft 16, 216)

Many of the plays stress the strength of this mortal passion, a passion which discarnate spirits, whose battles are less fierce, and therefore less passionate and life-giving, both fear and envy. In *The Shadowy Waters* the Fomorians become weak in the presence of "hearts that bend to love" (*DrC* 58-59), and Forgael's love for Dectora is a strong enough bond to protect Dectora from their grasp. *Deirdre*, which is in its final version primarily a play about mortal passion, documents the force of mortal love when it becomes hatred. King Conchubar, who has been jilted by Deirdre, plots to kill her lover Naoise and lures the lovers back to his kingdom by promising them clemency. Unhappily, the lovers believe him and return. The play argues that they were foolish to think that a love which had been so strong could diminish in strength when it turned to jealousy and hatred. The king's desire for revenge is so overpowering that it can only be quenched when his rival lies dead at his feet; it completely overshadows all sense of honour and justice. That this death also leads to Deirdre's death seems insignificant in comparison. Even in his grief at her death, Conchubar asserts that

> I, being King, did right
> In choosing her most fitting to be Queen,
> And letting no boy lover take the sway.
> (*VPl* 388)

The elaborate hierarchy of being which Yeats believed in, and which is represented by a vast array of spirits in the drama, can be understood as a chain linking the lowest creature in the universe to the highest, in "that universal mind, wherein every mood is a soul and every thought is a body" (*UP* I 247). Each spirit journeys down this chain and back up again, manifesting itself as every link in the chain in order to experience all knowledge, before it can return to the womb from which it was hurled at creation, the complete unity of which it is an integral part.

While undergoing this journey, the spirit is in constant conflict with spirits on all levels of being, for conflict is a manifestation of the division caused by creation, and cannot be overcome until all opposites are reconciled in the final unity. Conflict is in fact good and necessary, for through the struggle with its opposite/enemy, the spirit can eventually gain the knowledge and self-knowledge with which it will successfully negotiate its journey, and which will result in the elimination of conflict, the removal of desire, and the union with its Higher Self.

Though the plays centre on mortal protagonists, the struggles they depict are best understood in the context of this hierarchy of being, since many mortals in the plays either know, are told, or remember that they were once discarnate beings, and that their mortal garb will

3

"Bitter Memory": Forgetting, Acquiring Memories, and Remembering

The theme of memory, or more specifically of forgetting, acquiring memories, and remembering (dreaming back), is one of Yeats's favourite vehicles for integrating his theories about the nature and history of incarnate and discarnate spirits as unobtrusively as possible into the drama. This theme links a large number of the plays, for it figures prominently in such early works as *The Countess Cathleen*, *The Shadowy Waters*, and *The Wanderings of Oisin*, and grows in importance through *The Only Jealousy of Emer* and all the purgatorial plays right to *The Death of Cuchulain*. This theme is most readily understood by collating the references to memory in Yeats's philosophical treatises with those in early versions of the plays.

According to the philosophy thus pieced together, every spirit within creation goes through an almost interminable cycle of forgetting, learning, remembering, and forgetting, from its first descent into the gyres of time, through its journey around the phases of the lunar wheel, until its final return to the sphere of eternity. This cycle of forgetting and remembering is first undertaken by the spirit when it leaves the state of unity (innocence in Blakean terms) to journey through disparate experience, sampling separately every type of experience possible before integrating all of it into a greater innocence, a greater unity. This theory is beautifully illustrated in Yeats's poem "Shepherd and Goatherd," which describes the soul of Robert Gregory as it integrates the essence of the experiences of this life and then forgets its vehicle, memory, on its journey back to the beginning:

> "Jaunting, journeying
> To his own dayspring,

> He unpacks the loaded pern
> Of all 'twas pain or joy to learn,
> Of all that he had made.
> ....
> Knowledge he shall unwind
> through victories of the mind,
> Till, clambering at the cradle side,
> He dreams himself his mother's pride,
> All knowledge lost in trance
> Of sweeter ignorance."
>
> *(VE* 342-43)

The spirit first forgets its original unity, its complete self, at creation. It is left with a vague longing for unity which it seeks to quench by pursuing first one object of desire and then another down through the hierarchy of being. As part of this journey most spirits undertake a series of physical incarnations; before birth the spirit chooses – or has imposed on it by its destiny, those spirits who make up the external forces of the universe – the circumstances and personality into which it will be born. During its span on earth this personality accumulates a set of memories, memories that it truly believes in. Because life on earth is bitter, these memories are often painful, a curse as much as they are a blessing, and the soul (that part of the spirit which is incarnated) is torn between a desire to forget them, to shake itself free of these memories and this life, and a desire to cling to them, to believe in them as its sole reality.

Memory itself is specifically linked to mortality in the plays. Human beings have both memories and consciences, while discarnate beings have neither; "there's nothing will stop in their heads, / They've such poor memories, though they weep for it," says Aleel in *The Countess Cathleen* (*VP1* 55). Yeats stressed this point in his allegory, *The Cat and the Moon*, in which, as he claimed in the notes, "the blind man was the body, the lame man was the soul" (*VP1* 807). In the play the blind man, the body, *remembers* everything: "since I went blind in the tenth year of my age, I have been hearing and remembering the knowledges of the world" (*VP1* 796). The lame man, the soul, *forgets* everything: "Nothing stays in my head, Blind Man" (*VP1* 797), he laments.

Memory thus constitutes one of the most important differences between incarnate beings and discarnate spirits, and is a major cause of the conflict and rivalry between them. Many mortal protagonists in the plays envy spirits their freedom from sorrow and passion, from the pain and sheer weight of memories, which tie human beings to the earth perhaps more than anything else. Discarnate spirits, on the other hand, often envy people's memories, their record of actions, loves, and passions which the spirits, being without bodies, cannot enjoy: "deprived of the living present by death, they can create nothing, or, in the Indian phrase, can originate no new Karma" (*VP1* 968). "All power is from the body," Yeats wrote elsewhere, and they have only spirit. The daimons and teaching spirits who guide human beings through their destinies are said in *A Vision* to feed literally off human memories: "Our actions, lived in life, or remembered in death, are the food and drink of the *Spirits* of the *Thirteenth Cone* [the realm of the daimon in *A Vision*], that which gives them separation and solidity" (*AV* (B) 230).

This is just another facet of the ongoing struggle between this world and the "otherworld," its opposite, which characterizes Yeats's drama. Here, as always, mortals and disembodied spirits are living each other's death, dying each other's life. In play after play disembodied spirits, the so-called immortals, are imperfect beings existing at some stage between death and birth in which they have forgotten their old memories and have not yet picked up new ones. They need their opposites, human beings, and human memories in order to complete themselves. This is so in *The Only Jealousy of Emer*, to give but one example. Fand, so often taken to be a pure spirit who has never lived on earth, implies that she herself had once bodily form when she talks of being of those spirits who have *shed* their memories, who "all have washed out of their eyes / Wind-blown dirt of their memories / To improve their sight" (*VP1* 557). Significantly, it is Cuchulain's attachment to his memories which most infuriates her.

It is at death that the importance of memories becomes truly apparent. The soul must then face its memories, reliving them many times until they are understood and accepted. Only then can it integrate them into a new awareness of itself and thus be freed of them. The importance of this process cannot be overstated:

> Nor can there be work so great
> As that which cleans man's dirty slate.
> While man can still his body keep
> Wine or love drug him to sleep,
> ....
> But body gone he sleeps no more,
> And till his intellect grows sure
> That all's arranged in one clear view,
> Pursues the thoughts that I pursue,
> Then stands in judgment on his soul,
> And, all work done, dismisses all
> Out of intellect and sight
> And sinks at last into the night.
> ("The Man and the Echo" [1939], *VE* 632-33)

The purpose of life is understood in retrospect, after death, when the soul awakes from the drugged, sensual sleep that in the main characterizes mortality. For most spirits this understanding is arrived at slowly, through an often painful recreation of their earthly memories. This is purgatory, that state between lives that Yeats dramatized in plays as different as *Calvary*, *The Only Jealousy of Emer*, *The Words Upon the Window-Pane*, *The Dreaming of the Bones*, and *Purgatory* – in all these plays the disembodied spirits are obsessed with memories of their past lives, and struggle with varying degrees of success to free themselves from these mortal ties. Only after they have understood, accepted, and discarded their memories can these spirits join the purified spirits beyond purgatory, who are either between lives or who have escaped from the cycles of time entirely. This is the goal of all spirits, whether or not they are aware of it. "The *Spirit* is not those changing images . . . but the light, and at last draws backward into itself, into its own changeless purity, all it has felt or known" (*AV* (B) 220-21).

According to Yeats there is a possible obstacle in the way of achieving this goal which has nothing to do with the individual spirit – the memory of the living may interfere with the discarding of memory by the dead. In Yeats's world view "every mood is a soul and every thought is a body" (*UP* I 247), and, while the living are plagued by objects of sense, the dead are plagued by thoughts: "The toil of the living is to free themselves from an endless sequence of objects, and that of the dead to free themselves from an endless sequence of thoughts" (*M* 353-54). Because, as Yeats explained in "Per Amica Silentia Lunae," all the thoughts of the living take on a reality of their own which transcends time, a dead person may be unable to shake off this world, and its past existence within it, as long as there is someone here who remembers him or her. Said Yeats, somewhat facetiously, "it is for no other end that, all unknowing, we value posthumous fame" (*M* 359-60).

In another twist of his theory of memory, Yeats also believed that the collective memory of a group has as much reality as has the memory of the individual spirit. For this reason he placed great stock in the racial memory of the Irish people. He believed that the modern Irish needed, not to be freed of the memories of their past, but rather to be ransomed from their sordid present by the memories of their past greatness. He felt that this racial memory could be invoked (since no memory, though discarded by the spirits, is ever lost) and, in the poems and plays based on Irish mythology, actively sought to reawaken this memory in modern Irishmen, as he urged other poets to do:

Irish poets, learn your trade,
Sing whatever is well made,
Scorn the sort now growing up
All out of shape from toe to top,
Their unremembering hearts and heads
Base-born products of base beds.
Sing the peasantry, and then,
Hard-riding country gentlemen,
The holiness of monks, and after
Porter-drinkers' randy laughter;
Sing the lords and ladies gay
That were beaten into clay
Through seven heroic centuries;
Cast your mind on other days
That we in coming days may be
Still the indomitable Irishry.
                    ("Under Ben Bulben," *VE* 639-40)

Forgetting

At creation a community of spirits emerges from the original unity, each of whose members becomes aware of itself as a complete being, separate from and yet determined by the rest. Each spirit must now descend into the gyres or cones of time and space in order to be born. This descent is described more than once in *A Vision*, and is a theme of Yeats's poem "Chosen," in which lovers choose first to descend through the Zodiac (an alternate symbol in Yeats's work for the nine spheres of the Ptolemaic cosmology) to be born, and then to return after death to "the miraculous stream / Where – wrote a learned astrologer – / The Zodiac is changed into a sphere" (*VE* 535). The learned astrologer is Macrobius, and the passage to which Yeats alludes in the poem is the following:

Since those who are about to descend are yet in Cancer, and have not left the Milky Way, they rank in the order of the gods. . . . From the confine, therefore, in which the zodiac and galaxy touch one another, the soul, descending from a round figure which is the only divine form, is produced into a cone.[1]

F. A. C. Wilson explains this passage in his study of "Chosen":

In Platonism, the soul has a pre-natal existence in heaven, after which it descends through a series of stages into the material world, acquiring during its descent the attributes of personality it will have in its future life. The symbol used for the soul's abode before birth, as Yeats knew from Taylor's *Porphyry*,

---

1 Quoted from Thomas Taylor's *Porphyry* by F. A. C. Wilson in *W. B. Yeats and Tradition* (London: Methuen, 1968), p. 210.

was the Milky Way. From there, the soul descended, and the Platonists used the signs of the zodiac to symbolise the stages of the descent.[2]

As the spirit makes its descent through the spheres, or the signs of the zodiac, to be born, it must forget its true nature, its godliness, in order to believe completely in its personalities in successive lives. This leads to its separation into spirit and matter, or self and soul, or mortal and daimon, whose unresolvable conflict characterizes life. One of Yeats's favourite symbols for the spirit's first act of forgetting is Porphyry's "intoxicating cold drink of generation," which he explained in "The Philosophy of Shelley's Poetry":

> Cold, he [Porphyry] says, causes life in the world, and heat causes life among the gods, and the constellation of the Cup is set in the heavens near the sign of Cancer, because it is there that the souls descending from the Milky Way receive their draught of the intoxicating cold drink of generation.
>
> (*EI* 83)

Having drunk from this cup, the spirit loses its pre-natal memory. This cup is, of course, merely another variation on the streams, fountains, and wells of creation: the spirit drinks/drowns its way into material form.

In *Where There is Nothing* and *The Unicorn from the Stars* the intoxicating "cup of Lethe," as Yeats called it in *A Vision* (*AV* (A) 236),[3] makes its appearance through the psalm " 'Et calix meus inebrians quam praeclarus est!' How splendid is the cup of my drunkenness" (*VP1* 1106), which is one of the leitmotifs of the plays. In *Unicorn* the psalm is first used by Father John in reference to Martin's vision of the otherworld, the first half of which Martin remembers completely. In this vision Martin sees a number of unicorns (the soul, wrote Yeats in a letter [*L* 662]) who begin to trample on grapes, and it is here that his recollection fails him: "I smelt the wine, it was flowing on every side – then everything grew vague. I cannot remember clearly, everything was silent" (*VP1* 660).[4] Martin slowly recovers his memory of the vision, a little at a time, throughout the play, and finally remembers it

2 Wilson, *Yeats and Tradition*, p. 210.
3 In this passage, Yeats uses the symbol of the Cup of Lethe to explain the transformation of the soul in the last state between lives, when it must drink from the cup in order to erase its memory of its past life: "Whether it pass to a spiritual or to a human rebirth it must receive in the *Beatitude* – in Cancer – the Cup of Lethe. There all thoughts or images drawn from the *Faculties* during the *Shiftings* or the *Dreaming Back*, or that have remained in the *Faculties*, must be passed into the *Ghostly Self* [the Higher Self outside of time] and so be forgotten by the *Spirit*."
4 In his *Autobiographies*, Yeats described an experience which may have inspired Martin's vision. A friend of Yeats's went into a trance, during which he described an elaborate vision, but upon waking described an entirely different one, saying, " 'They gave me a cup of wine, and after that I remembered nothing' " (*A* 261).

in its entirety shortly before his death. The cup of drunkenness can thus be understood on one level of the play as a symbol of the spirit's forgetting of its spiritual nature, which it struggles to remember through its cycles on earth. On another level, the cup of oblivion is the world itself: "I saw a bright many-changing figure; it was holding up a shining vessel [*holds up arms*]; then the vessel fell and was broken with a great crash; then I saw the unicorns trampling it. They were breaking the world to pieces" (*VP1* 669).[5]

Refracting images of the shining vessel, that cold intoxicating cup, also pervade *The Player Queen*, where we find Septimus in the opening scene of the final version drunk, cold, and wet, "drenched with cold water, a whole jug of water, shivering in the pale light of dawn" (*VP1* 718).[6] Life, Septimus tells the countrymen, is merely a state "between two washings; for you were doubtless washed when you were born, and, it may be, shall be washed again after you are dead" (*VP1* 726); in an early version he states that "from water generation comes, but that's a mystery" (*MPQ* 221). This washing or bathing is at other times equated with drowning (most early versions of the play dwell on the symbol of spirits drowning into this life), at still others with drunkenness.[7] Yet life, this drunken state, is not necessarily bad – "I warn you against all sober men" (*VP1* 751), says Septimus. Decima prefers to play the part of Noah's drowned sister than that of Noah's wife who was saved by the Ark from drowning into material form. The cup of life is as full of love as it is of oblivion, and as such is indeed "splendid." Like most of the symbols in Yeats's plays, the cup works on several levels – its waters are bittersweet.

We must for a moment retrace our steps. Life is equated with memory, as we shall see, and as such has its rewards; it is also, however, equated with the *loss* of memory of other lives, other loves, the spirit's other (Higher) Self, and as such is very painful. Many of Yeats's plays, in particular *The Shadowy Waters*, *The Countess Cathleen*, and their companion poem *The Wanderings of Oisin*, are variations on the theme of forgetting. Porphyry's cup of forgetfulness is brought to mind in *The Shadowy Waters* by Forgael's "Harp of Forgetfulness," which he uses to destroy Dectora's memories of her dead lover Aleel and, even more

---

5 In the Cauldron ritual of Yeats's Celtic Mysteries, the Cauldron (one of the four treasures of the Tuatha de Danaan) is equated both with water and with creation: "In the outer man it is of water the procreant power of life in the inner. It has affinities with earth, with the stable images whose multiplication, as if reflected upon water, we call the creation of things" (*CMK* 254-55).

6 Note the similarity to the opening lyrics of *The Only Jealousy of Emer*, where the soul, now a "white frail bird," is flung out of the sea at daybreak (*VP1* 529).

7 For a more detailed discussion of the theme of drowning in *The Player Queen*, cf. Chapter 4, "Chance."

tenacious, her memories of Aengus and the gods of light. Forgael plays on the harp and sings,

> O love be forgotten as the soul forgets
> the spirit when the body overwhelms it.

and

> O bright gods be forgotten as you
> are forgotten when the soul enters the world.
>   (*DrC* 65-66)

Forgael is a mortal, though a half-god, who has been deprived of the effect of the cup of forgetfulness by being granted a wisdom generally denied human beings. This wisdom teaches him two truths that others blissfully forget when they enter their bodies. The first is that life constitutes a separation from one's own spirit, and is a mere passing of time until the soul can be reunited with itself. This is the same secret which Owen Aherne learns in "The Tables of the Law," to his unending despair: "I have seen the whole, and how can I come again to believe that a part is the whole? I have lost my soul because I have looked out of the eyes of the angels" (*M* 306). Like Aherne, Forgael can find no meaning in life, because he has been shown that it is merely illusion, a series of images which mortals mistake for the truth; it is the "dream" from which the Wise Man awakes at the end of *The Hour-Glass*. The second truth revealed to Forgael, which deepens his despair, is that many ages, many successive, interminable lives separate mortals from the end, and thus from the final rest.

The Shadowy Waters focuses on waiting, killing time, and forgetting. All the gods and all the men who surround Forgael engage in various forms of forgetting. The Fomor pass the time by pillaging, and urge Forgael to do the same:

> Loosen the grey sails out upon the winds
> And overwhelm white cities and forget.
>   (*TPBS* 6)

The sailors are lulled to sleep by the Harp of Forgetfulness, through

> A music that can quell all elements
> And creatures and make memory lie down
> Asleep under a purple coverlet
> Of indolent dreams.
>   (*TPBS* 13)

Dectora and Aleel pass the time by dreaming and loving (we are reminded of Yeats's statement in "The Man and the Echo" that "While man can still his body keep / Wine or love drug him to sleep"

[*VE* 633]); that their love is just another way of forgetting is signalled by the fact that Aleel in more than one pre-1900 version of the play charms Dectora into loving him by playing three notes on the magic harp (*TPBS* 12). The Danaan gods also "dance upon the mountain tops / And sing in the deep valley and forget" (*DrC* 149). Aengus himself, in some versions of the play, lulls himself into this same forgetfulness through a series of languorous dreams (*DrC* 246).

Forgael alone is denied forgetfulness. He can neither hate enough to fight like the Fomor, nor, try as he might, can he believe in his dreams like Aengus. Various early manuscript versions focus on Forgael's elaborate attempts to induce Danaan dreams in himself. In an early pre-1896 version, for example, Forgael orders the Fomor to steal apple blossoms from Aengus's "island of the young" (*DrC* 80); with them he attempts to induce these dreams of forgetfulness:

> (O sweet odour of apple blossoms, that is in my nostrils,
> give me some divine passions, some hatred,
> some love, that I may forget how many
> > me
> ages divide from the white sleap when
> all things shall have come to an end.
> O grant that I may love & hate like
> the gods before I die. ~~& know forgetfulness~~
>
> > > (*DrC* 82)

In other pre-1900 versions he attempts to induce these same dreams by lying on crushed roses which he has stolen from the Island of the Danaans, but, though these dreams "do not awaken desire and unquiet" (*DrC* 213) in the Danaans, they only arouse "shadows of desire: a pearl white hound" (*DrC* 142) in Forgael. Even Forgael's courting of Dectora is, at least on one level, merely another attempt to forget ("he forgets his [loneliness] when he looks at her [Dectora]" [*TPBS* 48]), and it is only in the final versions, when Yeats was trying to simplify his play, that Forgael's motivation actually becomes a quest for love. It is thus fitting that Forgael should be so obsessed with the destruction of creation, and he sails, though with "the tiller" swaying "listlessly . . . / above his head" (*DrC* 213), towards the end of the world:

> > his sorrows are as loud
> > > his galley drifts
> > As any march bird, & ~~he heads his galley~~ (sic)
> > Among the empty waves where the world ends.
> > > > (*DrC* 87)

In other plays the protagonists, while they are not as acutely aware as is Forgael that life constitutes a sham and an illusion, a forgetting of the original unity which is reality, are nevertheless riddled by the same "shadows of desire," vague longings which cannot be satisfied by this life. These are symbolized in the plays by "fleeing phantoms of desire," the white hound chasing the deer, the young man chasing the woman with a golden apple in her hand. Yeats equated these phantoms with those seen by Rousseau, in Shelley's *The Triumph of Life*, after the Morning Star gives him a drink from a cup "full of oblivion and love" which returns him to *life*; "He drinks and his mind becomes like sand 'on desert Labrador,' marked by the feet of deer and a wolf" (*EI* 89). Yeats continues, "Because the wolf is but a more violent symbol of longing and desire than the hound, his wolf and deer remind me of the hound and deer that Oisin saw in the Gaelic poem chasing one another" (*EI* 90). Once the memory of self is gone the spirit is left with a vague desire, which defines life; it is a desire for what the spirit lost at creation, but takes on various guises, all illusion, as the spirit chases it through the realms of time and space.

The longing for immortality, or the desire for the love of immortals which is manifested by Oisin, by Forgael in some versions of *The Shadowy Waters*, and by Cuchulain throughout the Cuchulain cycle, seems a vague memory of humanity's rightful spiritual condition. This seems to be Yeats's interpretation of desire, which he based on an oft-quoted passage by Leonardo da Vinci: "this longing is in its quintessence the spirit of the elements, which finding itself imprisoned within the life of the human body desires continually to return to its source" (*Memoirs* 88, n. 3). Cuchulain's meeting with the goddess Fand in *The Only Jealousy of Emer* certainly corroborates this interpretation. This meeting, which is set in some region outside time, functions on a number of levels, as proof that Yeats could indeed transmit his complex metaphysics more completely through verse and ritual than through abstract thought, and memories of Cuchulain's pre-natal and earthly existences figure prominently in them.

On one level Cuchulain is merely dreaming, but a dream so powerful that his wife Emer can actually see it unfolding before her. This is a re-enactment of Yeats's poem "An Image from A Past Life," in which the wife sees the image-rival which haunts her husband in dreams, though he forgets the image in his waking state. She cries,

> A sweetheart from another life floats there
> As though she had been forced to linger
> From vague distress
> Or arrogant loveliness,
>
> (*VE* 390)[8]

8 Yeats accompanied this poem with elaborate notes, in which he explained that "in moments of excitement images pass from one mind to another with extraordinary

In *The Only Jealousy of Emer* the dream image, Fand, has been haunting Cuchulain all his life, as can be gathered from Lady Gregory's *Cuchulain of Muirthemne*, which provided the story line for this play, and by early versions of the play, in one of which Fand asserts that "Since you were born / I have been close at hand / now dim now bright / Waxing and waning as your sight was turned / Towards me or away."[9] Her haunting may well explain his waking dissatisfaction with mortal women, and thus his roving from one to another. Fand reminds him of this dissatisfaction, saying,

> But what could make you fit to wive
> With flesh and blood, being born to live
> Where no one speaks of broken troth.
> (*VPl* 557)

Yeats wrote that dream images, particularly passionate ones, are drawn from memories of a state before birth, memories that the soul forgets in its waking state. "Souls that are once linked by emotion never cease till the last drop of that emotion is exhausted — call it desire, hate or what you will — to affect one another . . . this ideal form becomes to the living man an obsession, continually perplexing and frustrating natural instinct" (*VE* 822-23). Cuchulain in his dream may thus be remembering his spirit-lover from another life; on another level, however, he is remembering, as must Aengus in his dreams, his other self before time and separation. Yeats made this very explicit in early drafts of the play, through the recurring image, abandoned in the final version, of Cuchulain as the white, Fand as the yolk, of an egg that was broken by his birth into time.[10] There is a parallel in *The King of the Great Clock Tower* where the stroller, though he is encased in a gross bodily form and has forgotten his origin, seeks out the queen from out of time, his beloved, and demands union with her. When he is decapitated, the queen moves before him in a dance which symbolizes their union, and his soul, reunited with its Higher Self, begins to sing. Fand's dance before Cuchulain should have the same meaning, except that Cuchulain, because more strongly attached to this world than is the stroller, and because his true opposite or daimon, now that the beloved is within reach, has become Bricriu, must reject Fand and thus the completion symbolized by the dance.

ease, perhaps most easily from that portion of the mind which for the time being is outside consciousness" (*VE* 823).

9 Stephen R. Winnett, "An Edition of the Manuscripts of Two Plays by W. B. Yeats, *The Only Jealousy of Emer* and *Fighting the Waves*" (Ph.D. Dissertation, New College, Oxford, 1978), p. 73.

10 Winnett, "Manuscripts of Two Plays," p. 51.

There is an even more compelling reason why Cuchulain must reject Fand. She is asking him to accept her kiss in exchange for oblivion, for the relinquishing of the memories of his life. Here, as in many other plays, the theme of forgetting is linked not only to the soul's forgetting of its divinity, but also to the forgetting of the painful memories of this life.

Acquiring Memories

Yeats's protagonists are torn between the desire to escape the memories of this life and the desire to cling even to the most painful of these memories. This vacillation, between the desire to escape life, and the knowledge that what human beings prize the most is part and parcel of the mortal condition, is a central theme of several of Yeats's plays, and is articulated by two musicians in discarded opening lyrics to *The King of the Great Clock Tower*, a play *about* life in time. While the first musician feels very deeply the mockery that is time and memory, and longs for the stroke of midnight, a symbol in this play for the end of time, the second musician understands that "All love is shackled to mortality."

FIRST MUSICIAN:
> I wait until the tower gives forth the chime;
> And dream of ghosts that have the speech of birds;
> Because they have no thoughts they have no words;
> No thought because no past or future; Time
> Comes from the torture of our flesh, and these,
> Cast out by death and tethered there by love,
> Touch nerve to nerve throughout the sacred grove
> And seem a single creature when they please.

SECOND MUSICIAN:
> I call to mind the iron of the bell
> And get from that my harsher imagery,
> All love is shackled to mortality,
> Love's image is a man-at-arms in steel;
> Love's image is a woman made of stone;
> It dreams of the unborn; all else is nought;
> Tomorrow and tomorrow fills its thought;
> All tenderness reserves for that alone.[11]

The spirit begins to acquire its temporal memories, the record of its actions and passions, as soon as it enters this life, and its main task in this life is to live as fully and exhaustively as possible. As Yeats wrote in

11 Quoted by Allan Wade, ed., *The Letters of W. B. Yeats* (New York: Macmillan, 1955), p. 817.

the notes to *The Resurrection*, "Even though we think temporal existence illusory it cannot be capricious; it is what Plotinus calls the
characteristic act of the soul and must reflect the soul's coherence"
(*VP1* 934). While Yeats argued in his more optimistic plays that one of
the main reasons for living is to accumulate and savour the memories
of this life, these same memories figure prominently both as a blessing
and as a curse in Yeats's drama. Through them Yeats worked into the
plays what Richard Ellmann describes as

the two forces he had always seen at work in the world, the one regarding
reality as temporary, provisional, tidal, the other regarding it as hive- or
nest-like, tenacious, lasting. "Let all things pass away," says a world-
conqueror in "Vacillation," while in *A Vision* Yeats quotes with approval an
impromptu song of Iseult Stuart, "O Lord, let something remain."[12]

The memories of life are not altogether despised by even those
protagonists who, like Cuchulain, are tempted to escape them. The
memories of love in particular are often described as shackles which
keep people from their freedom, and yet they are clung to tenaciously.
Dectora won't forget her love for her dead husband Aleel in *The
Shadowy Waters*, Emer refuses to give up her love for her estranged
husband in *The Only Jealousy*, even the poet Aleel in *The Countess
Cathleen*, though he longs to escape this world, cannot renounce his
one tie to it, his love for Cathleen. Though Deirdre says, near the end of
her life, that she knows nothing "but this body, nothing / But that old
vehement, bewildering kiss" (*VP1* 376), the first kiss that Naoise gave
her, it is enough to have made her tragic life worthwhile. When the
musicians speculate that "though you have suffered all for mere love's
sake / You'd live your lives again," Deirdre answers, "Even this last
hour" (*VP1* 378).

Discarnate spirits, in envying men their memories, long for what
gives men the most pain, perhaps, but also the fire of passion. With
words that could easily be spoken by any of the immortals who are
attracted to mortals in the plays, a faery explains to Hanrahan in *The
Secret Rose* why she loves him: "I have loved you from the night I saw
you lying on the Grey Rath, and saw you turning from side to side, for
the fire in your heart would not let you rest. I love you, for you are
fierce and passionate and good and bad and not dim and wave-like as
are the people of the Sidhe."[13] In *The Countess Cathleen* there are several
references to spirits who envy human beings their memories, and
bewail their own lack of them. Thus we are told the story of Queen

12 Richard Ellmann, "At the Yeatses," *New York Review of Books*, May 17, 1979, p. 25.
13 W. B. Yeats, "The Book of the Great Dhoul Hanrahan the Red," in *The Secret Rose*
(London: Lawrence and Bullen, 1897), pp. 138-39.

Maeve, a goddess of the Sidhe, who mourns every full moon, not for the death of the mortal man she loved nine centuries before, but because she cannot remember his name. "So she loves truly," says Cathleen when she is told of Queen Maeve's sorrow. Not so, answers Aleel, for she "but wets her cheeks / Lady because she has forgot his name" (*VP1* 55). In the same play, the souls of the dead, who carry off Cathleen's treasure under duress in early versions of the play, mourn that they won't remember tomorrow their bad conscience of today:

> 1ST SPIRIT:
> I'll never dance another step, not one.
> 2ND SPIRIT:
> Are all the thousand years of dancing done?
> 3RD SPIRIT:
> How can we dance after so great a sorrow?
> 4TH SPIRIT:
> But how shall we remember it tomorrow?
> 5TH SPIRIT:
> To think of all the things that we forget.
> 6TH SPIRIT:
> That's why we groan and why our lids are wet.
> (*VP1* 127)

Memory can be understood as a metaphor for life in this world, with its inescapable joy and pain. Many mortals, Yeats emphasizes, are quite satisfied with the "dance" of this life, with the joys of home, hearth, and children. Thus Aibric pleads with Forgael to return home to "be some fair woman's friend" and "live like other men" (*VP1* 321), while in *On Baile's Strand* Cuchulain is urged by his companions to abandon his reckless ways "to live in comfort" (*VP1* 512), to settle down with wife and children. The musicians at the end of *At the Hawk's Well* sing,

> "The man that I praise,"
> Cries out the leafless tree,
> "has married and stays
> By an old hearth, and he
> On naught has set store
> But children and dogs on the floor.
> Who but an idiot would praise
> A withered tree?"
> (*VP1* 413-14)

The implication is that it is dangerous and foolhardy to attempt a different life from that meant for human beings, to search for a knowledge beyond the realm of mortality. The rewards for those who succeed may be great, but the perils for those who, like the Old Man in *At the Hawk's Well*, do not succeed are even greater.

One man who exemplifies the acceptance of this life and its memories is Maurteen in *The Land of Heart's Desire*. This simple little allegory pits this world, represented by Maurteen, his wife, and the local priest, against the world imagined by young dreamers, in this play Maurteen's daughter-in-law Mary. Like Michael in *The Speckled Bird*, who longs to change the world and "remake it nearer to the heart's desire" (*SB* 22), Mary is attracted by the "otherworld," represented in this play by the Faery Child. Maurteen understands her longings, but argues that she will soon outgrow them, even as he has:

> (... have not Fate and Time and Change
> Done well for me and for old Bridget there?)
> . . . .
> This is the best of life; (when we are young
> We long to tread a way none trod before,
> But find the excellent old way through love,
> And through the care of children, to the hour
> For bidding Fate and Time and Change good-bye.)
> (*VP1* 190)

The Faery Child explicitly equates Maurteen's life with memory, saying,

> Your memories have made you wise, old father;
> The young must sigh through many a dream and hope,
> But you are wise because your heart is old.
> (*VP1* 197-98)

Faeryland is free of memory, says the Child, "for we are but obedient to the thoughts / That drift into mind at a wink of the eye" (*VP1* 206). This is what attracts Mary to Faeryland; like Forgael and later Cuchulain, she feels oppressed by everything that Maurteen's life represents. He has, she says, "a kind tongue too full of drowsy love, / Of drowsy love and my captivity" (*VP1* 192). Mary chooses to leave her husband's family and home to journey to Faeryland with the Child. As she prepares to leave, her husband Shaun attempts to seduce her into staying, using as bait the memories of their life together: "Remember when I met you by the well," says Shaun, "And took your hand in mine and spoke of love" (*VP1* 208).

The irony in this is evident; the world of hearth and home is a trap, even though it is recommended for most mortals in the plays, and its accompanying memories are a curse that Mary is justified in trying to escape. The rebellion against this life and the struggle to escape its memories which is dramatized in one form or another in most of

Yeats's plays is clearly more valuable than the simple acceptance of "the excellent old way" demonstrated by Maurteen. This is keeping with Yeats's continuing insistence that conflict is necessary to life and growth. As he wrote in *A Vision*: "My instructors identify consciousness with conflict, not with knowledge [Maurteen's 'wisdom'], substitute for subject and object and their attendant logic a struggle towards harmony, towards Unity of Being" (*AV* (B) 214).

Nevertheless, most of Yeats's plays argue that outright escape from the cares of the world is not the answer. The futility of such a choice is particularly emphasized in *The Wanderings of Oisin*, *The Countess Cathleen*, and *The Only Jealousy of Emer*, three plays which focus on the ties of memory. In *The Wanderings of Oisin*, Oisin escapes the world, with its memories of sorrow and pain, to follow his ideal love, Niamh, to three different faery worlds. He discovers, not the spiritual paradise he was expecting, but instead three different types of dances that the disembodied spirits engage in to forget. The first island, the Isle of Dancing, is the kingdom of light of the Tuatha de Danaan, the land of perfected spirits who run together and sing together in perfect harmony. But though its inhabitants continually dance and celebrate, there is no discernible motive for their revelry. Indeed, when Oisin picks up a harp to sing of the joys of the human world, they are overcome by intense sorrow and can only rid themselves of it by taking his harp and throwing it away. "Things that have grown sad are wicked" (*VE* 20), they cry, and plunge into revelry once more. Aengus exhorts them to be joyful, for " 'joy is God and God is joy' " (*VE* 19), but he himself dreams and forgets. This world cannot still Oisin's memories for long, and he grows nostalgic for the world of time, as he recounts to St. Patrick:

> When one day by the tide I stood,
> I found in that forgetfulness
> Of dreamy foam a staff of wood
> From some dead warrior's broken lance:
> I turned it in my hands; the stains
> Of war were on it, and I wept,
> Remembering how the Fenians stept
> Along the blood-bedabbled plains,
> Equal to good or grievous chance:
>
> (*VE* 24)

Niamh now takes him to a world of unending battles, "an island of endless battle for an object never achieved" (*VP1* 932), but this island is worse still, for it is but a parody of life within creation, with its constant conflict between unreconcilable opposites. Oisin fights for a hundred years with the same god; they fight, the god dies, Oisin rests, the god reappears, and they must begin once again. This episode is in fact reminiscent of *The Herne's Egg*, also in many ways a parody both of human life and of men's aspirations.[14] In *The Wanderings of Oisin*, the third island, "the Island of Forgetfulness," is the most horrifying of all, for there all pretense is abandoned; it is populated by grotesque beings who sleep away eternity in order to dream and forget. Niamh and Oisin lie down beside them and fall asleep in their turn; says Oisin, "gone like a sea-covered stone / Were the memories of the whole of my sorrow and the memories of all of my mirth" (*VE* 52).

As they wander from one island to another, Niamh, though she, unlike Oisin, has no memories with which to contrast these islands, grows gradually more sorrowful, and when Oisin asks her "and which of these / Is the Island of Content?" she weeps and answers, "None know" (*VE* 46). Far from being the paradise of immortals (though unaccountably understood by many critics as a paradise which Oisin is too grossly mortal to appreciate), these islands are merely variations of mortal life and of the many lives human beings will have to endure before the end of creation, while the dances of forgetting engaged in by immortals are merely variations of Oisin's own attempts to escape his memories. Yeats even confessed in the notes to *The Resurrection*, many years later, "How hard it was to refrain from pointing out that Oisin after old age ... would pass in death over another sea to another island" (*VP1* 932). Oisin remains in each island one hundred years, and always his memories, though of the sadness of the world, "the ancient sadness of man" (*VE* 54), call him back, or force him to move on. Finally, he says, "Remembrance, lifting her leanness, keened in the gates of my heart" (*VE* 52), and he is compelled to leave Niamh and return to Ireland.

Those among Yeats's protagonists who attempt to escape this world do so at the risk of gaining, not release from pain and sorrow, but merely oblivion. This is stressed in *The Countess Cathleen* which, particularly in the versions of 1895 and after, centres on the theme of forgetting. Memories reinforce the predicament of the incarnate spirit, for it has to balance vague, unspecified longings which cannot be satisfied in this world with its memories, which attach all men, often

14 *The Herne's Egg* opens to the sound of fighting; it is the fiftieth battle between King Congal and King Aedh, but they are so evenly matched that they expect to fight fifty more. Only at the end of the play does Congal realize the utter uselessness of it all, and tells the Fool,

> Never be a soldier, Tom;
> Though it begins well, is this a life?
> If this is a man's life, is there any life
> But a dog's life?
>
> (*VP1* 1038)

despite themselves, to the world of conflict, of good and evil. This is stated most explicitly by the Devils in *The Countess Cathleen*, who promise freedom from conflict and from the cares of the world in exchange for the souls of mortals. They promise

> Wine that can hush asleep the petty war
> Of good and evil, and awake instead
> A scented flame flickering above that peace
> The bird of prey knows well in his deep heart.
>
> (*VP1* 37)

In another version their promise is even more appealing, for they contrast the peace that they offer, and that they claim all discarnate spirits, whether good or evil in life, have attained, with the tumult of the world:

> Is that peace
> Known to the birds of prey so dread a thing?
> They, and the souls obedient to our master,
> And those who live with that great other spirit
> Have gained an end, a peace, while you but toss
> And swing upon a moving balance beam.
>
> (*VP1* 132-34)

The Devils' offer in *The Countess Cathleen* seems all the more attractive because the burdens of the world are so onerous that everyone, including Cathleen, has been attempting to forget them right from the beginning of the play. When the play opens, Cathleen, on her doctor's advice, is retreating from the world to her castle: "I was bid fly the terror of these times / And wrap me round with music and sweet song / Or else pine to my grave" (*VP1* 21). Her castle seems to offer the peace and forgetfulness that the devils offer the peasants, for it is "A place that's set among impassable walls / As though the world's trouble could not find it out" (*VP1* 17). Significantly, Cathleen has difficulty in finding her castle, and finds instead famine and fear "Where I had thought I would find nothing changed" (*VP1* 19).

Cathleen now turns to sleep, to dreams, to the songs offered by the poet Aleel in the search for forgetfulness. When Aleel tells her a story about the troubles of the Sidhe goddess Maeve, Cathleen says, "She'd sleep that trouble away . . . / If she had better sense" (*VP1* 55). Sleep, like the sleep of forgetfulness of the third island of *The Wanderings of Oisin*, is constantly brought up in the later versions of this play through Oona, Cathleen's guardian, who urges Cathleen to sleep until the problems are over and is continually grateful for the sleep and forgetfulness of old age. The bard Aleel sets little store by memory, and tries by various means to get Cathleen to forget hers:

What's memory but the ash
That chokes our fires that have begun to sink?
And they've [the spirits] a dizzy, everlasting fire.
                                                    (*VP1* 57)

In some versions he even has a harp which he uses, as Forgael and
Aleel do in *The Shadowy Waters*, to weave dreams of love and forgetting.
Cathleen is almost seduced, and is tempted to escape with him and his
harp to Faeryland, to "dwell among the Sidhe / In their old ever-busy
honeyed land" (*VP1* 62). Aleel also offers Cathleen his love, and it is
this that tempts her most of all to forget her responsibility to the welfare
of the peasants. Nevertheless, she finally chooses to face this responsibility, protesting that she is

tired of tympan and harp,
And tired of music that but cries sleep, sleep,
Till joy and sorrow and hope and terror are gone.
                                                    (*VP1* 53)

The Only Jealousy of Emer focuses more than any other play on the
strength of the ties of memory, and it is in this play that Yeats makes his
most convincing case for the value of these memories. As the play
opens, Cuchulain is in a trance, in a state somewhere between life and
death, and Fand comes to him in this state to seduce him into escaping
with her into the other world. Cuchulain wavers, because he is very
much a mortal, tied to this earth by memories which he is reluctant to
forget. When Fand first approaches him he is crouched on the floor, as
though clinging to the earth. She asks, "What pulled your hands about
your feet, / Pulled down your head upon your knees," and he answers, "Old memories" (*VP1* 551-53). He longs to escape with her and
thus forget the memories of the son he has killed, of the woman whose
trust he has violated, but he cannot bring himself to do so. Fand is
surprised by the strength of his memories, and argues that he deserves
better. In this she resembles Niamh, who cannot understand why
Oisin insists on turning "his gaze / On the old sorrows of his human
days" (*VE* 29).

Fand tries to persuade Cuchulain to kiss her, stating that her kiss will
grant him freedom from memory, and thus freedom from his conscience, from "Intricacies of blind remorse." For Fand this kiss will
represent completion, union with her opposite within time. Scholars
have long argued that this kiss would have signalled completion, and
therefore release from the wheel of time, for Cuchulain as well. In an
unpublished Ph.D. dissertation H. A. Reeves follows conventional
wisdom in arguing that Cuchulain would have been better off kissing
Fand, and bases this on the fact that "the image of the kiss as emblem-

atic of the union of opposites, completion of the round of being, is frequently used in the later plays."[15] This may be so, but Fand comes specifically to obtain completion for herself. She offers Cuchulain in return merely "oblivion":

> When your mouth and my mouth meet
> All my round shall be complete
> Imagining all its circles run;
> And there shall be oblivion
> Even to quench Cuchulain's drought,
> Even to still that heart.
>
> (*VPl* 555)

A study of the evolution of this play reinforces this point. Fand's kiss is merely a refined version of the "helmet of forgetfulness," very much like the Harp of Forgetfulness featured in *The Shadowy Waters* and in *The Countess Cathleen*, that the Woman of the Sidhe offers Cuchulain in the earliest drafts of the play to "save . . . [Cuchulain] from memory."[16] S. Winnett, the editor of these early drafts, writes that "This somewhat clumsy device would later be replaced by the much more elegant (and structurally balancing) kiss of forgetfulness."[17]

> WOMAN OF THE SIDHE:
> Take it, but there is no enemy to beat down
> It is the helmet, ~~of lies~~ of forgetfulness, & these
> these little shelly things that cover it, are the wing
> cases of the beatle of forgetfulness. When
> the dead place it upon their head, any
> regret vanishes with memory.[18]

Like Cathleen, Cuchulain hesitates, then refuses the drug of forgetfulness, saying,

> Take again your helmet – have you not
>   dread
> known that the ~~thought~~ of forgetting, is the greatest
> pang of life – what death is there like that
> death – to so forget who one loves, is not
> a death of the body but of the soul . . .[19]

In these very early versions it is quite clear that it is Fand, and not Cuchulain, who is to be pitied. He is racked by the pain of his life and

15 H. A. Reeves, "The Dramatic Effectiveness of Yeats's Imagery in the Later Plays" (Ph.D. Dissertation, University of North Carolina, 1968), p. 100.
16 Winnett, "Manuscripts of Two Plays," p. 117.
17 Winnett, "Manuscripts of Two Plays," p. 65.
18 Winnett, "Manuscripts of Two Plays," p. 69.
19 Winnett, "Manuscripts of Two Plays," p. 70.

loves, but he is very much alive, while she, "Being separate from the
flesh is but a dream / And therefore miserable."[20]

In later versions published in the variorum edition of the plays the
strength of Cuchulain's memories continues to be emphasized, and
though he sympathizes with Fand, saying,

> How could you know
> That man is held to those whom he has loved
> By pain they gave, or pain that he has given
> Intricacies of pain,

he refuses to give them up:

> What dread so great as that he should forget
> The least chance sight or sound, or scratch or mark
> On an old door, or frail bird heard and seen
> In the incredible clear light love cast
> All round about her some forlorn lost day?
>
> (*VP1* 559)

Cuchulain thus refuses to kiss Fand, and she is about to send him off to
Manannan for punishment when Emer renounces his love for her and
breaks Fand's hold on him, thereby releasing him to return to earth. It
is only in the final version of the play that Cuchulain gives in to Fand,
and it is up to Emer, in a scene which greatly strengthens the drama, to
save him from the consequences of his decision. It is ironic that Emer,
who valued only two things on earth, the memory of Cuchulain's love
and the hope that this love will one day be reinstated, must give up this
hope as Bricriu's condition for restoring Cuchulain to life. He comes
back to the arms of his mistress, and Emer is left alone with her
memories.

Though escape from the pain of life is offered in many guises in the
plays, in the form of Faeryland, or the peace of oblivion, or the love of
immortals, it is shown to be inadequate in all the plays save perhaps
The Land of Heart's Desire. The only truly effective method of shedding
the memories of earth while still in the body, which would lead not
merely to oblivion but to unity of being, is taught by Paul Ruttledge in
Where There is Nothing. Not surprisingly, since this is the play most
indebted to Yeats's magical studies, and resembles in many respects
the rituals for his Celtic Mysteries, Paul reiterates the method taught by
Yeats's magical order. Paul leaves his family, his possessions, even his
identity, detaching himself from every bond that holds him to this
earth, to make his heart and mind "as bare as the wilderness"
(*VP1* 1141), and he urges his followers to do the same. According to

20 Winnett, "Manuscripts of Two Plays," pp. 52-53.

J. M. Rist, this is the very method which Plotinus taught for achieving union with the One:

> The one is pre-eminently simple – to attain likeness to it we too must be pre-eminently simple. Hence Plotinus' cry through all the stages of the "mystic way" is the more insistent here [in the *Enneads*]: "Strip away everything"; "put away all shape"; "the man who lets every Form go will see." If we see the One by being like it, and the One itself is unspeakable and hard to tell of, we ourselves can hardly expect to see it if we are still characterized by the finite forms.[21]

The One is the whole, the undivided self, while the self during time is by definition divided, since it is characterized by memories which Yeats equates in his essay, "The Mandukya Upanishad" with a fragmented spirit, "forgetting, remembering, sleeping, waking, spread out into past, present, future" (*EI* 480). Since memories are a by-product of desire, it follows that the object of desire must be relinquished before these memories can be shed and spirit can be made whole.

Nevertheless, as Yeats implies in "Per Amica Silentia Lunae," this relinquishing of desire while in the body is a rather difficult step for most human beings to take.

> I think that we who are poets and artists, not being permitted to shoot beyond the tangible, must go from desire to weariness and so to desire again, and live for the moment when vision comes to our weariness like terrible lightning, in the humility of the brutes. . . . Only when we are saint or sage, and renounce experience itself, can we, in imagery of the Christian Cabbala, leave the sudden lightning and the path of the serpent and become the bowman who aims his arrow at the centre of the sun.
>
> (*M* 340)

While Yeats would argue that it is possible for any man to follow Paul's advice and reach perfection and thus release from the wheel of time in any one life, for most mortals the letting go of the ties of memory which Paul advocates is a much lengthier process. It takes place during purgatory, in the state immediately following death, when the spirit must "remember" the memories of life by reliving them over and over again until it has learned from them and accepted them fully. Only then is it free to forget them.

Remembering (Dreaming Back)

> And shall I never know again
> Intricacies of blind remorse?
> (*VPl* 555)

21 J. M. Rist, *Plotinus: The Road to Reality* (Cambridge: Cambridge University Press, 1967), p. 134.

After death, wrote Yeats in "Per Amica Silentia Lunae" and in "The Soul in Judgment" chapter of *A Vision*, the spirit leaves the terrestrial condition and enters "the condition of air where images have but a borrowed life, that of memory" (*M* 357). The ghost now dreams itself through six different states between lives before it is ready for reincarnation or, if it is sufficiently perfected, for release from the wheel of time: "Neither between death and birth nor between birth and death can the soul find more than momentary happiness; its object is to pass rapidly round its circle and find freedom from that circle" (*AV* (B) 236). The first three of these states are molded by the memories of its past life; they resemble life in that they also represent "no orderly descent from level to level, no waterfall, but a whirlpool, a gyre" (*AV* (B) 40), and the ghost must move back and forth between them until it has fully relived and expiated its memories.

> We carry to *Anima Mundi* our memory and that memory is for a time our external world; and all passionate moments recur again and again, for passion desires its own recurrence more than any event, and whatever there is of corresponding complacency or remorse is our beginning of judgment; nor do we remember only the events of life, for thoughts bred of longing and of fear... come again like a rope's end to smite us upon the face.
>
> (*M* 354)

Because thought *is* existence in this condition, the memories as well as the fears and doubts of the soul, now a ghost, form a reality that it believes in completely, even as it believed completely in its mortal existence on earth. Says Dr. Trench in *The Words Upon the Window-Pane*, one of several plays devoted to unravelling existence between death and life, "Some spirits are earth-bound – they think they are still living and go over and over some action of their past lives, just as we go over and over some painful thought, except that where they are thought is reality" (*VPl* 944). The object of the exercise is for the soul to confront and fully accept the memories of its previous life. In this state it must work through them all, recollecting them first with all their passion and fury, and then in tranquillity, as it were, dwelling on them until their full significance, their causes and effects, have been understood, and until all the emotion which they give rise to has been exhausted. "All that keeps the *Spirit* from its freedom may be compared to a knot that has to be untied or to an oscillation or violence that must end in a return to equilibrium" (*AV* (B) 226).

The spirit in the first three states between lives in Yeats's metaphysics is therefore in a purgatorial state, but one that differs somewhat from Christian tradition, as Helen Vendler points out: "the question is never 'I did this, and I repent and will do otherwise,' but, 'Did I do this?' – tracing each action to the source, measuring the lot, forgiving himself (when he can) the lot. To become *impassive* in the face of one's remembered experience is the Yeatsian goal, not to repent and do otherwise."[22] Because for Yeats good as well as evil are merely opposites which must ultimately be reconciled, the ghost in the third state must also be "purified of good and evil. In so far as the man did good without knowing evil, or evil without knowing good, his nature is reversed until that knowledge is obtained" (*AV* (B) 231).

Purgatory in Yeats's view is purely self-created; it is short if the soul is purposeful, its conscience clear, but it is interminable if the soul is fearful or wracked with guilt about actions and thoughts in its past life. Thus Yeats often cited the case of a ghost in a Japanese play who burned for ages in a self-created hell as retribution for what it felt was an evil life on earth, and who could not be freed from the burning flames of this hell until it stopped believing that they were real. In the same way characters like the mother in *Purgatory* cannot be freed to continue their spiritual journey until they stop rejecting, denying, or being entranced by these memories – they must learn to contemplate them with indifference.

Were Cuchulain to have escaped life through death in *The Only Jealousy of Emer* (and this can be understood to have taken place on another level of the play, though Emer later calls him back to life, because he is referred to as one of those dreaming shades who "when they dream no more return no more")[23] the purging of his memories would have been lengthy and traumatic, for he would have been beset by recurring nightmares such as of killing his own son, the memory of which ties him to earth in *The Only Jealousy of Emer*. C. G. Jung, Yeats's contemporary in age and thought, wrote that the spirit can leave this life with the least trauma "when life has been lived so exhaustively, and with such devotedness, that no more unfulfilled obligations to life exist, when, therefore, no desires that cannot be sacrificed unhesitatingly stand in the way of inner detachment from the world."[24] In *The*

22 Helen Vendler, "Changing Metaphors for the Otherworld," *Modern Drama* 7 (1964), p. 309, n. 2.
23 In the earliest drafts, Cuchulain is several times referred to as already among the dead. Bricriu says to Emer,
      "~~Your~~ The longing and ~~your~~ the cries have drawn him here
      And made him dream himself in to the form
      That is familiar to him – for after death
      That form awakes when ever the heart is stirred"
      (Winnett, "Manuscripts of Two Plays," pp. 48-49)
24 C. G. Jung, "Commentary," in Richard Wilhelm, trans., *The Secret of the Golden Flower: A Chinese Book of Life* (2d ed.; New York: Harcourt, Brace, and World, 1957), p. 114.

Only Jealousy of Emer, Cuchulain cannot yet bring himself to renounce his desires and his memories of this life — he is in the middle of life and knows nothing but life. In *The Death of Cuchulain*, on the other hand, Cuchulain is now an old man who has played out his life fully and completely and is ready, even eager, for death. His purgatory is thus short and painless. "The more fully a life is lived," wrote Yeats in *A Vision*, "the less the need for — or the more complete is — the expiation" (*AV* (B) 236).

Like *The Only Jealousy of Emer*, *The Death of Cuchulain* can be understood on more than one level. On the most literal level Cuchulain is of course approaching his death. On another level, however, Cuchulain seems already to have passed beyond life and begun the expiation which is necessary before he can discard his memories and become pure spirit. Very near death after receiving his first mortal wound, Cuchulain seems in a daze, and says "Where am I? Why am I here?" (*VP1* 1057). He begins to dream the dreams of a shade, and all the important events and memories of his life, simplified for dramatic purposes, pass before his eyes. First he remembers the events dramatized in *The Only Jealousy of Emer* (*VP1* 1055); next he sees Aoife, the woman who fought him in *At the Hawk's Well* and bore the son he killed in *On Baile's Strand*. Although she is now as old as he is, he at first mistakes her for the young woman he fought and conquered so long before, and imagines himself still at the scene of the original confrontation:

> You fought with a sword,
> It seemed that we should kill each other, then
> Your body wearied and I took your sword.
>
> (*VP1* 1057)

She has to remind him that "that time was long ago / And now it is my time. I have come to kill you." Suddenly he remembers the series of events following their first meeting:

> And now I know your name,
> Aoife, the mother of my son. We met
> At the Hawk's Well under the withered trees.
> I killed him upon Baile's Strand...
> You have a right to kill me.
>
> (*VP1* 1057)

Other memories float before his eyes, but they fade rapidly away, and just before dying Cuchulain sees the shape he will assume when he is dead, not the body which endured the crises of his mortal existence, but

My soul's first shape, a soft feathery shape,
And is not that a strange shape for the soul
Of a great fighting-man?

(*VPl* 1060-61)[25]

That he goes to join the company of disembodied spirits freed of their separateness and memories, those spirits which have reached the last stage of the life between death and birth, is made clearer in Yeats's poem "Cuchulain Comforted," a companion piece to the play written shortly after *The Death of Cuchulain*. In the poem Cuchulain, now dead, is approached by a number of spirits, "bird-like things," who have lost their individuality on the road to perfection. As they explain to Cuchulain, " 'We thread the needles' eyes, and all we do / All must together do' " (*VE* 634). They are clearly in the fifth state between lives, the Purification, which is inhabited, as Yeats wrote in *A Vision*, by daimons and guiding spirits such as his own communicators: "in piecing together [their] detached statements, I remember that some spirit once said to me: 'We do nothing singly, every act is done by a number at the same instant.' Their perfection is a shared purpose or idea" (*AV* (B) 234). In the poem the spirits in unison hand Cuchulain a shroud, his *Celestial Body*, which once donned will obliterate the *Passionate Body* of mortal life. As F. A. C. Wilson speculates in his study of the poem, Cuchulain accepts the shroud, and by the end of the poem has been transformed into a bird and joined the spirits in their collective song: "They had changed their throats and had the throats of birds" (*VE* 635).[26]

In *Calvary*, *The Words Upon the Window-Pane*, *The Dreaming of the Bones*, and *Purgatory*, on the other hand, the dead do not escape mortality so easily. These plays in the main dramatize variations on the second state between lives, called alternately the "dreaming back" and the "return":

25 Note the resemblance to the human-headed birds, the souls of the recently dead, who lead Forgael to the end of the world in later versions of *The Shadowy Waters*.
26 This is a very difficult poem which has led to confusing interpretations, particularly F. A. C. Wilson's, who argues both that it symbolizes Dante's "Valley of the Negligent Rulers," peopled by spirits "Outside true purgatory; granted the ease they sought in life, their punishment is the desire they feel for active purgation" (*Yeats and Tradition*, p. 246) and that it represents a community of "pure souls, who have escaped from the round of birth and death" (p. 248). The most logical explanation, I would propose, is that the poem represents Cuchulain's union with his spiritual daimons which, because they are his opposites, are "convicted cowards all" since he was a warrior; they are nonetheless purified spirits, though perhaps still in the final stages between death and life (*AV* (B) 234), and lead him quickly through the purging and discarding of his passionate body.

In the *Dreaming Back*, the *Spirit* is compelled to live over and over again the events that had most moved it; there can be nothing new, but the old events stand forth in a light which is dim or bright according to the intensity of the passion that accompanied them. They occur in the order of their intensity or luminosity, the more intense first, and the painful are commonly the more intense, and repeat themselves again and again. In the *Return*, upon the other hand, the *Spirit* must live through past events in the order of their occurrence, because it is compelled by the *Celestial Body* to trace every passionate event to its cause until all are related and understood, turned into knowledge, made a part of itself.

(AV (B) 226)

These purgatorial plays depict various ghosts who are trapped near the earth by the memories of crises or crimes in their past lives of which they have not been able, for different reasons, to purge themselves.

Christ in *Calvary* can be understood at least on one level of the play to be already among the dead. On this level he is, like Jonathan Swift in *Words Upon the Window-Pane*, reliving three crises in his past life; like Swift, he is so caught up by the strength and pain of his memories that he does not know that he is dead. Christ in this play is akin to the subjective heron (his opposite) of the opening lyrics who "shivers in a dumbfounded dream" in which he stares at his own reflection in the water, the symbol of matter in which the spirit is reflected or, in this case, imprisoned. He cannot escape reliving his crucifixion and certain events preceding it because, as H. Vendler notes, he has not accepted his rejection by Lazarus and Judas and the soldiers at the cross.[27] Chant the musicians,

> He climbs up hither but as a dreamer climbs.
> The cross that but exists because He dreams it
> Shortens His breath and wears away His strength.
> *(VP1* 781)

Christ is held near the earth by his memories in the same way that Lazarus is trapped in the world by the life Christ restored to him. Lazarus, Like Forgael and so many other Yeatsian protagonists, would have preferred the death Christ took from him, or at least a waste space "where there is nothing" (*VP1* 783), and cannot forgive Christ for returning him to life:

> Alive I never could escape your love,
> And when I sickened towards my death I thought,
> "I'll to the desert, or chuckle in a corner,
> Mere ghost, a solitary thing." I died
> And saw no more until I saw you stand
> In the opening of the tomb.
> *(VP1* 782-83)

27 Vendler, "Changing Metaphors," pp. 315-16.

Christ remembers his rejection by Lazarus, by Judas, and by the dice-throwers. He will not be able to purge himself of these images until he can accept the fact that he could not save all men and consequently, what must be the most painful truth of all for a Saviour, that he is only one of many gods – "If he were but the God of dice he'd know [the dance of dice-throwers]... , but he is not that God" (*VP1* 787).

In *The Words Upon the Window-Pane* it is Jonathan Swift who is tortured because he has not come to terms with specific incidents in his past life. This is the play most obviously influenced by Yeats's long-standing affiliation with the Society for Psychical Research. It takes the form of a séance organized by the Dublin Spiritualists' Association and attended by psychical investigators, a skeptical scholar, and several believers. During the séance a medium, one Mrs. Henderson, is taken over by a control personality, "a dear little girl called Lulu who died when she was five or six years old. She describes the spirits present and tells us what spirit wants to speak" (*VP1* 946). Because this play is written in prose and is dominated by the rational, probing intellects of Dr. Trench and Mr. Corbet, it is much more literal and straightforward than most of Yeats's plays. Here the ghost of Jonathan Swift, who has disrupted several previous séances, appears; he is a fairly conventional ghost haunting, as one would expect, a house in which he once lived.

Swift is re-enacting, we are told, exactly the same scenes, with exactly the same words, as he has in two previous séances and, we must assume, many more times in the last two centuries, as if he were an actor, says the medium, "in some kind of horrible play" (*VP1* 943). Swift is reliving crises which occurred at three different times in his life, first with Vanessa, when she pleaded with him to have children, then with an aging Stella, and finally that brought on by his own senility and degeneration. This is the most important crisis, and so the filthy, diseased, and senile body of his old age dominates the play, both at the beginning, when the spirit child Lulu sees him crouched in the corner of the room (*VP1* 947), and at the end, when the medium awakens to see him "dirty, his face covered with boils. Some disease had made one of his eyes swell up, it stood out from his face like a hen's egg" (*VP1* 955). But because the ghost takes on the body it inhabited when it underwent the different crises, this senile old man alternates with a younger, more impressive figure. Writes Douglas Archibald,

There is great tension between the three images of Swift. The public figure imagined and discussed by Corbet is at the height of his power; the man loved by Stella and Vanessa is past his prime but not yet sunk "into imbecility or madness"; the aged, deformed and demented apparition is the dying dean of legend and fact. . . . His Swift is the most powerful, the most fully rendered, of Yeats's images of despair and suffering.[28]

In another purgatorial play, *The Dreaming of the Bones*, the ghostly protagonists appear as young and handsome lovers because their story and the crisis that they are attempting to expiate began when they were young. Unlike Swift, Diarmuid and Dervorgilla have committed a serious crime, and thus their purgatory is more clearly defined and better understood by the ghosts, who are aware that they are dead and yet unblessed. They know that other, more fortunate shades, who merely "Warred in the heat of blood" have long since forgotten their earthly memories and been united with their former enemies (opposites) of this world:

> They and their enemies . . .
> Mix in a brief dream-battle above their bones;
> Or make one drove, or drift in amity;
> Or in the hurry of the heavenly round
> Forget their earthly names.
>
> (*VP1* 770)

Diarmuid and Dervorgilla's penance, on the other hand, has lasted for seven centuries. The young mortal protagonist, astounded by the length of their purgatory, asks, "What crime can stay so in the memory?" (*VP1* 772).

The lovers "sold their country into slavery" (*VP1* 773) by aiding the Norman invaders. The crime is not forgotten because the spirits themselves have not forgotten it, or forgiven themselves for their part in it. Tortured by their own consciences, they wander forever together and yet apart, for every time they are about to seek comfort in a kiss, they remember their crime and avert their faces. Yeats writes that, like the ghost in the Japanese play mentioned earlier, "The Lovers in my play have lost themselves in a different but still self-created winding of the labyrinth of conscience" (*VP1* 777). The first step towards release will be accomplished when they realize that the torture *is* self-created. There is, however, an added complication, which adds to the length of their penance. The nature of the crime is such that though it took place seven centuries before, its consequences are still being felt by the living, who themselves refuse to accept the crime and forgive the criminals. Diarmuid and Dervorgilla's names and story are known and shuddered at by living Irishmen like the Young Man who listens to

28 Douglas Archibald, "*The Words Upon the Window-Pane* and Yeats's Encounter with Swift," in Robert O'Driscoll and Lorna Reynolds, eds., *Yeats and the Theatre* (Toronto: Macmillan of Canada, 1975), p. 198.

their story in the play. Though moved to pity by their plight, he refuses to forgive them and free the pair from their responsibility in the crime, and thus from their memory of it. He remembers the crime with as much bitterness as if it were freshly committed, and says, "O never, never / Shall Diarmuid and Dervorgilla be forgiven" (*VP1* 773). Because the horror of the crime lives as freshly in the minds of the living as of the dead, the ghosts are doomed to wander until some one among the living decides to forgive their crime and thus set their conscience to rest.

The influence of the living on the memories of the dead is of even greater thematic importance in *Purgatory*. At first reading, the purgatory of the title seems to be that of the dead mother, now a ghost, who haunts the house of her youth and relives, time and time again, her honeymoon night. Her son, now an Old Man, watches as she stands by the window of the house, waiting for her husband:

> She has gone down to open the door.
> . . . .
> She is mad about him. They mount the stairs.
> She brings him into her own chamber.
> And that is the marriage chamber now.
>
> (*VP1* 1046)

Her son speculates that "she must live / Through everything in exact detail, / Driven to it by remorse" (*VP1* 1046), remorse caused by the knowledge that the product of their union would grow up to hate his mother and murder his own father. The Old Man is obsessed by his parents' crimes, his mother's in betraying her house and heritage by marrying a stable hand, his father's in seducing her, dissipating her fortune, and tormenting his own son until he was driven to parricide:

> I stuck him with a knife,
> That knife that cuts my dinner now,
> And after that I left him in the fire.
>
> (*VP1* 1045)

The Old Man knows that he plays a large role in his mother's torment, and hopes that he can help free her from her tortured memories. As he explains to his son, all spirits in purgatory must

> Re-live
> Their transgressions, and that not once
> But many times; they know at last
> The consequence of those transgressions
> Whether upon others or upon themselves;
> Upon others, others may bring help,

> For when the consequence is at an end
> The dream must end.
>
> (*VPl* 1042)[29]

The Old Man decides to help his mother to escape her purgatory by killing his own son, thus stopping the consequence of her actions from being perpetrated on another generation. Needless to say, he does not succeed. Though the boy is dead at the end of the play, his mother continues to await her lover in the haunted house. We are left to wonder if her memories will indeed fade when she accepts and expiates them herself, when "she has purified her own memory of all emotion," in F. A. C. Wilson's words,[30] or if her escape must await her son's own acceptance of them. Should this be the case, the poor woman's release will be slow in coming; the Old Man will have to forgive and forget through a purgatory of his own, not just her actions but the consequences of her actions, his own murders first of his father and now of his only son.

There is another possibility: the dead woman's torment may have been precipitated by the Old Man's memories, and not by her own. On second reading, it becomes apparent that the true purgatory in the play is being experienced not so much by the mother as by the Old Man himself. It is he who is obsessed by his memories, obsessed by the haunted shell of his house. He has come by before; this time he has brought his son, and begins to relive the life of that household:

> I think about its jokes and stories;
> I try to remember what the butler
> Said to the drunken gamekeeper
> In mid-October, but I cannot.
> If I cannot, none living can.
>
> (*VPl* 1041)

As the Old Man's memories grow more vivid and more personal, the old house is slowly brought to life until even the Old Man's son, who at first thinks him crazy for insisting that the house is lit up, can see the figures wandering through it. It is also the Old Man, and not his mother, who is the most obsessed with her "marriage chamber." He is tortured by the inevitability of his parents' union:

> Do not let him touch you! It is not true
> That drunken men cannot beget,
> And if he touch he must beget
> And you must bear his murderer.
>
> (*VPl* 1046)

---

29 This is of course a distortion, through a madman's eyes, of Yeats's theory of purgatory.

30 Wilson, *Yeats and Tradition*, p. 147.

He is tortured also by the knowledge that she may be drawn back, not so much by remorse, as he hopes, but by memories of pleasure:

> and yet
> Can she renew the sexual act
> And find no pleasure in it, and if not,
> If pleasure and remorse must both be there,
> Which is the greater?
>
> (*VPl* 1046)

He is tortured, finally, by the knowledge that she died in childbirth. As a direct consequence of her "crime," her son has become a murderer thrice over, first of his mother, then of his father, and finally of his only son. It is therefore not only up to the mother to unpack "the loaded pern" (*VE* 342), it is up to the tormented son to "Measure the lot; forgive . . . [himself] the lot" ("A Dialogue of Self and Soul" [*VE* 479]).

A variation on the Old Man's view of purgatory is dramatized in *The Player Queen*, though in this play the subject of purgatory is treated rather more playfully. In draft sixteen of the manuscript versions the ghost of the dead king appears and, speaking through a beggar, bemoans his sinful ways. He prays that his daughter will set a better example than he did, and punish the sins of his countrymen, thus putting an end to the sinning of his people which is the direct consequence of his own evil ways. Only then will his soul find peace. He cries, "Must I wander always in Purgatory for my sins; must I endure pains when I thought my daughter had put all to rights? Obey my daughter, I say, then I shall be forgiven my sins" (*MPQ* 220).

Such is purgatory. The spirit reaches the fourth state, the Marriage or Beatitude, only after it has freed itself from its memories: "All memory has vanished, the Spirit no longer knows what its name has been, it is at last free and in relation to *Spirits* free like itself." Yeats continues, "The *Spirits* before the Marriage are spoken of as the dead. After that they are spirits, using that word as it is used in common speech" (*AV* (B) 235). It is at this stage that, as Yeats asserted in the 1925 edition of *A Vision*, the spirit once again drinks from the cup of forgetfulness in order to prepare itself to enter the next phase of its existence. "Whether it pass to a spiritual or to a human rebirth it [the spirit] must receive in *Beatitude* – in Cancer – the Cup of Lethe. There all thoughts or images . . . must be passed into the *Ghostly Self* [the permanent self] and so be forgotten by the *Spirit*" (*AV* (A) 236). In the next two states the spirit, now a clean slate, readies itself for a different incarnation or, if it has sufficiently perfected itself, returns to the One.

Postscript

A number of knots in Yeats's theory of memory remain to be untied. First of all it seems that while we, the living, remember the dead, they continue to exist in their past form. Yeats claimed in "Per Amica Silentia Lunae" that ghosts of long-dead men, regardless of the state of their conscience at death, continue to hover near the earth as long as someone on earth remembers them: "the famous dead, and those of whom but a faint memory lingers can still – and it is for no other end that, all unknowing, we value posthumous fame – tread the corridor and take the empty chair" (*M* 359-60). It is this reason that Decima, the player Queen, gives for wishing to die after she is crowned queen in draft six of the manuscript versions of that play:

> A moment, an hour I am part of the world
> And when I am dead shall be mourned a queen.
>
> (*MPQ* 54)

Posthumous fame is the sole reward that Cathleen Ni Houlihan offers to those who help her fight for Ireland:

> They shall be remembered for ever,
> They shall be alive for ever,
> They shall be speaking for ever,
> The people shall hear them for ever.
>
> (*VPl* 229)

Nevertheless, these memories of the living will not necessarily impede the departed spirit from achieving peace and continuing into other existences, for the memories of the dead which linger after the spirit has accepted and shed its memories, and which must continue to linger while they are remembered by the living, are merely the shell or husk of these discarded memories (*M* 359); it may be that the ghost who haunts the ruined house in *Purgatory* is not the tortured spirit of the woman but the abandoned husk of her passionate body given breath again by the memories of her son. The magical tradition to which Yeats paid allegiance did in fact believe that we are surrounded by discarded husks of memory of all departed spirits, husks which float in the astral plane, and it frowned upon spiritism for this reason (though Yeats ignored the warning), feeling that evil spirits may well enter these empty shells of memory and use them to deceive mortals attempting to communicate with the dead. The magician Maclagan adds another twist to this in a relevant passage of Yeats's unfinished novel, *The Speckled Bird*: "These [spirits] were but images drawn out of his memory and made to live by wandering spirits who inhabited them, and he began to explain an intricate theory of the relation between this world and the other. The God of the angels and Swedenborg's writings were but memories, too. They were memories or symbols" (*SB* 69).

Conversely, when the living forget the dead, the latter begin to fade away. Yeats claimed that this is what happened to the Irish gods, who lost their past stature when the Irish people ceased to believe in them, and were reduced to the faeries who haunt the countryside. "Quite beyond any doubt," he wrote, "many of them were long ago gods of Ireland" (*UP* I 137) but, since they "can but appear in forms borrowed from our limited consciousness" (*UP* I 247), "They have gradually dwindled in the popular imagination until they have become the Faeries" (*VE* 796). Yeats tried all his adult life to revive this belief in the ancient gods of Ireland, first through the establishment of Irish Mysteries based on the ancient Druidic mysteries, which AE called "the noblest of all Earth's memories" (*Candle* 65).

The Celtic Mysteries project was abandoned by 1902, and Yeats turned to his drama with renewed vigour in an effort to obtain the same result by recreating the ancient Irish myths and giving life to the heroes and gods of Ireland. He hoped that the modern Irish would follow his example and, by remembering their past, their heritage, restore life and breath to these myths. In the mythological plays Yeats attempted to awaken the racial memory which shaped Ireland; in other more bitter plays, such as *The Words Upon the Window-Pane* and *Purgatory*, he mourned the demise of the aristocratic class of Ireland which kept the best of Irish traditions, and hence its racial memory, alive.

The last knot, once untied, leads to Yeats's beliefs on free-will and determinism. Yeats believed that, while the living may influence the forms which the dead can assume, they themselves are influenced by the memories of their ancestors, by the collective memory, that is, of all spirits who once thought. This belief was also held by C. G. Jung, who wrote that,

Although we human beings have our own personal life, we are yet in large measure the representatives, the victims and promoters of a collective spirit whose years are counted in centuries. We can well think all our lives long that we are following our own noses, and may never discover that we are, for the most part, supernumeraries on the stage of the world theater. . . . Thus at least a part of our being lives in the centuries.[31]

Yeats stated his belief in a collective memory, "the memory of Nature herself" (*EI* 28), in his essay "Magic," and reiterated it in "The Philos-

31 C. G. Jung, *Memories, Dreams and Reflections*, trans. R. and C. Winston (New York: Random House, 1965), p. 91.

ophy of Shelley's Poetry," where he spoke of "the sudden conviction that our little memories are but a part of some great Memory that renews the world and men's thoughts age after age, and that our thoughts are not, as we suppose, the deep, but a little foam upon the deep" (*EI* 79). It is this memory of nature which is, Yeats continued, "the dwelling-house of symbols, of images that are living souls" (*EI* 79). This collective memory, the memory of our ancestors, stored, it may be, within nature herself, forms the objective reality of the universe; every action, every thought is retained in the collective memory (though the original thinker may have forgotten it) and only when all spirits forget, or stop perceiving, will this universe dissolve. Yeats stated this explicitly in a passage in the 1925 edition of *A Vision* which illuminates further his position as both a realist and an idealist:

Berkeley thought if his study table remained when he closed his eyes it could only be because it was the thought of a more powerful spirit which he named God, but the mathematician Poincaré considers time and space the work of our ancestors. With the system in my bones I must declare that those ancestors still live and that time and space would vanish if they closed their eyes.

(*AV* (A) 158).

It is only a short step from this statement to "The Seven Propositions," where Yeats describes "reality" as a community of spirits, and says, "When these Spirits reflect themselves in time and space they still determine each other, and each Spirit sees the others as thoughts, images, objects of sense. Time and space are unreal." The spirits who are perceived by the individual spirit as "thoughts, images, objects of sense" are thus the collective memory which influences the memory, as well as the actions, of the individual spirit. Since the community of spirits determines, to some extent, the individual spirit, the former is in a sense the latter's destiny:

The dead living in their memories are, I am persuaded, the source of all that we call instinct, and it is their love and their desire, all unknowing, that make us drive beyond our reason, or in defiance of our interest it may be; . . . and in their turn, the phantoms are stung to a keener delight from a concord between their luminous pure vehicle and our strong senses.

(*M* 359)

In the words of AE, whose chapter "The Memory of Earth" echoes Yeats's convictions on the subject, "We soon grow to think our memory but a portion of that eternal memory and that we in our lives are gathering an innumerable experience for a mightier being than ours" (*Candle* 56). This "mightier being" is, AE later explained, no more and no less than "ourselves beyond this mirage of time and space by which we are enchanted" (*Candle* 148).

4

"He Burns the Earth as if He Were a Fire": Chance, Choice, and the Spiritual Seeker in the Drama

In the notes to *Calvary*, Yeats hinted that the issue of chance and choice is the cornerstone of his philosophy. He quoted an old Arab, a follower of Kusta ben Luka on whose teachings Yeats claimed that *A Vision* was based, who explains that "Kusta ben Luki [sic] has taught us to divide all things into Chance and Choice; one can think about the world and about man, or anything else until all has vanished but these two things, for they are indeed the first cause of the animate and inanimate world" (*VP1* 790). The relationship of chance to choice is examined by Michael Robartes, Yeats's alter ego, in the opening sequence to *A Vision*, where he remarks to his friends, "I found myself upon the third antinomy of Immanuel Kant, thesis: freedom; antithesis: necessity; but I restate it. Every action of man declares the soul's ultimate, particular freedom, and the soul's disappearance in God; declares that reality is a congeries of beings and a single being" (*AV* (B) 52). That freedom and necessity are equal forces is reiterated in "The Seven Propositions," Yeats's late summary of his metaphysics in which the problem of destiny is particularly stressed; Yeats stated that "Though the Spirits are determined by each other they cannot completely lose their freedom." However, Proposition V underscores that the struggle of the incarnate spirit to maintain its freedom in the face of the forces of destiny is the most difficult, and important, struggle in human life.

These forces of destiny are the spirits who make up the "stream of souls" which is the universe, and who collectively determine, and are determined by, the individual spirit. Since, as Yeats wrote in "Per Amica Silentia Lunae," "All power is from the terrestial condition, for there all opposites meet and there only is the extreme of choice possi-

ble, full freedom" (*M* 356), the struggle between the will of the individual spirit and the forces of destiny is at its most bitter in human life.
The struggle for mastery between chance and choice is another variation of the conflict between mortals and immortals in the drama,
opposites "That have been hatreds for three times the age of / This
long 'stablished ground" (*VP1* 478). The difference is that the conflict is
now on a much larger scale. The forces of chance, from creation
onwards, wield tremendous power over human beings in many of the
plays, as we have already seen. They take on various forms, appearing
now as "God," Manannan, or the Great Hearne, now as the forces of
generation and destruction which God has at his command. In the
manuscript versions of *The Player Queen*, for example, these forces of
chance appear as cycles of violent destruction which can annihilate the
world at any time. At other times they appear as the cycles of history
which supersede the cycles of the individual spirit, as the repressive
forces of a particular age which the individual spirit must either accept
or rebel against, and as the spirit's opposite, that being he loves and
hates the most.

A large number of protagonists in the drama feel the influence of
destiny at some point in their lives, as often as not through a personal
intervention which manifests itself in dreams, or in waking visions and
trances (the border between the two worlds which has a psychical, as
much as a physical, reality). This destiny, wrote Yeats in "Per Amica
Silentia Lunae," is in fact their daimon.

> I think that all religious men have believed that there is a hand not ours in the
> events of life, and that, as somebody says in *Wilhelm Meister*, accident is
> destiny; and I think it was Heraclitus who said: the Daimon is our destiny.
> When I think of life as a struggle with the Daimon who would ever set us to the
> hardest work among those not impossible, I understand why there is a deep
> enmity between a man and his destiny, and why a man loves nothing but his
> destiny.
>
> (*M* 336)

The struggle between chance and choice unfolds on many levels in
the plays. It is often developed through images of fire and burning
which are linked both with the larger forces of chance and with the
choice of the individual mortal; these images have broad ramifications
in the drama. Fire is one of the most powerful symbols of ungovernable
force, and the forces of chance (God's choice) and choice (God's
chance) are the unquantifiable elements in Yeats's system, capable of
wreaking chaos amidst its order. For Yeats water connotes generation,
the gushing forth of the fountain of creation; fire on the other hand
connotes destruction, for it is equated with the "condition of fire
[which] is all music and rest" (*M* 357) at the end of creation, and with

the "fires of the last day" which will destroy creation.[1] With reference to individual spirits, water is the "heart," the mortal passions, but fire is the "soul" (*L* 826), that which existed before creation and which will continue to exist after it. Following the pattern already uncovered in the plays, images of fire and burning occur more frequently than those of water and flooding, given the greater concern of Yeats's protagonists with the destruction of creation. The struggle between the forces of free-will and determinism, which will inevitably lead to a reconciliation of these forces and thus to an end of "the world" and "man" (*VPl* 790), is simply another variation of this longing for destruction.

The Player Queen and its companion plays, *The Unicorn from the Stars* and *Where There is Nothing*, hint rather broadly at a coming cataclysm in Yeats's own time, the destruction of the world by fire to succeed the Deluge, the original destruction/creation by water. Unlike the Flood, the fiery cataclysm may well signal the annihilation of creation. Since these images of light, fire, and burning are associated everywhere in Yeats's work with the "otherworld" in its various guises, this destruction by fire may mean the end of the world as we know it, through a spiritual fire which will destroy it in order to effect a return to the beginning. This is the fire referred to by the Brother in Yeats's short story "Where There is Nothing," when the child asks him, "Why is the ruby a symbol of the love of God?" Answers the Brother, "Because it is red, like fire, and fire burns up everything, and where there is nothing, there is God" (*M* 185).

However, even if the world is not physically destroyed, humanity will nevertheless be changed, for the cataclysm will certainly bring about spiritual regeneration: it is linked in the plays to the prophecy of a second coming, of a new god who will announce a new subjective and, for Yeats, spiritually enlightened age to succeed the decaying objective age brought about by the coming of Christ. There is a sense of prophetic urgency attached to Yeats's introduction of this theme in his work, for he, like many of his friends and associates, passionately believed in the coming changes. In the words of AE: "Out of Ireland will arise a light to transform many ages and people. There is a hurrying of forces and swift things going out and I believe profoundly that a new Avatar is about to appear and in all spheres the forerunners go before him to prepare."[2]

---

1 In the "spear" ritual of Yeats's Celtic mysteries the three initiators represent the three types of fire: "The First Initiator speaks of 'the green fire of the grass' ['vital fire' cancelled] and fire in the sense of life. The Second Initiator speaks of destroying fire, the blackness in the flame, the terrible scorching heat. The Third Initiator (not showing his face) speaks of the Fire Beyond (only a few words)" (*CMK* 189).

2 AE, *Passages from the Letters from AE to W. B. Yeats* (Dublin: Cuala Press, 1936; rpt. 1971), p. 17.

Images of fire, appropriately enough, are also used to describe the relationship of the individual to his or her personal destiny. The daimon comes to the individual in a flash of "sudden lightning" (*M* 361) such as Yeats described in "Vacillation" and again in "Per Amica Silentia Lunae," when, sitting in a restaurant, his mind suddenly became "pure and far extended and so luminous that the images from *Anima Mundi*, embodied there and drunk with that sweetness, would, like a country drunkard who has thrown a wisp into his own thatch, burn up time" (*M* 365). This is but a momentary taste of the condition of fire, where all is made clear and lucid, and where mortal and daimon are finally united. Guided by their daimon, some mortals will make the necessary choices for attaining this condition relatively quickly, while others take a much longer time, which is why some go through the cycles of time so much faster than others, and why, though all journeys began together at creation, there are now, according to Yeats, spirits in every phase of existence. Nevertheless, the final consequence of this battle with the more personal forces of destiny, as with its larger forces, is ultimately spiritual regeneration, an alchemical process transforming the soul and leading to the final blazing consummation of the union with the daimon in the condition of fire.

Yeats stated in "Per Amica Silentia Lunae" that the greatest conflict, and therefore the greatest choice, occurs in the mortal condition. This is echoed in a number of plays and in *The Wanderings of Oisin* where Oisin, having travelled to the island of the immortals who mock "at Time and Fate and Chance" (*VE* 20) and live "Unchainable as the dim tide, / With hearts that know neither law nor rule" (*VE* 22), feels more than a little constrained by the pressure to be joyful, the only choice in that condition, and longs for the opportunity to battle once more with "good or grievous chance" (*VE* 24). However, Yeats also warned that true freedom is no more the victory of choice over chance than it is the escape from these forces of chance; true freedom is instead the reconciliation of these two forces, a reconciliation normally associated with unity of being at the end of division.

Yeats's concept of freedom in the mortal condition is thus more than a little complex. Human beings are free on earth, and yet determined by spirits who, it is implied, have chosen this life and this character for them; they are free and yet bound to travel through twenty-eight phases of the lunar wheel and countless phases between lives. Moreover, human beings, it now appears, are most free when most determined by their fate, for the closer they come to accepting (or choosing) their rightful destiny, the freer they become. Yeats argued in the plays, as will be seen, that those who rebel against the forces of chance and choose complete freedom must, paradoxically, be led by the forces of chance in the end. Only those who are content to struggle with fate, without any hope of winning (as are some *antithetical* mortals) and those who accept this fact completely, believing that "one day one loses and the next day wins" (*VP1* 786) (as do some *primary* mortals), can truly reconcile chance and choice, and therefore most easily escape the conflict.

Yeats wrote in *A Vision*, "all that keeps *Spirit* from its freedom may be compared to a knot that has to be untied or to an oscillation or a violence that must end in a return to equilibrium" (*AV* (B) 226). While all incarnate spirits have some degree of freedom, for "consciousness is choice" (*AV* (A) 131), true freedom is this "return to equilibrium" sampled temporarily by the spirit in the discarnate phase of the lunar wheel, Phase 15, where "Chance and Choice have become interchangeable without losing their identity" (*AV* (A) 70), and in the later states between death and life, and found permanently in God, or in the unity beyond division. The notes to *Calvary* reinforce this argument. There an old Arab states that only in God can the two forces of chance and choice be reconciled: "In God alone, indeed, can they be united, yet each be perfect and without limit or hindrance" (*VP1* 790). In "All Soul's Night" Yeats implied that this reconciliation of chance and choice in "God" is the goal of all spirits in their journey through creation. Referring to the late Florence Farr he wrote that,

> much had she ravelled out
> From a discourse in figurative speech
> By some learned Indian
> On the soul's journey. How it is whirled about,
> Wherever the orbit of the moon can reach,
> Until it plunge into the sun;
> And there, free and yet fast,
> Being both Chance and Choice,
> Forget its broken toys
> And sink into its own delight at last.
>   (*VE* 472-73)

The ongoing battle with the forces of destiny in the mortal condition thus becomes not a struggle for mastery so much as a struggle for transcendence, for perfection. Since this union beyond the confines of time and space is sought as eagerly by the forces of destiny as by the individual spirit, these forces will lead that spirit to make the choices which will lead to spiritual transcendence. Yeats commented on Shakespeare's plays that "I feel in Hamlet, as always in Shakespeare, that I am in the presence of a soul lingering on the storm-beaten threshold of sanctity. Has not that threshold always been terrible, even crime-haunted?" (*Memoirs* 233). This is certainly at least as applicable to his own plays, since the bitter struggle between the forces of freedom and necessity which is ultimately for spiritual perfection takes place on just such a border, now a "threshold of sanctity," between the incarnate and discarnate worlds.

Images of light and fire are used to present the choices open to the seekers in the drama for dealing with these forces of chance;[3] the most extreme choice, attempted by Martin Hearne of *The Unicorn from the Stars*, is to burn down the world and consume the bonds of mortality in order to set himself free. Martin is set apart from mortals such as Thomas in that play who are content to settle for the comfort of love and family within the confines of mortality, and his choice is ultimately a spiritual one, as are most of the choices which Yeats drew attention to in the drama. Though they are slightly different for the rebel, like Martin, the saint, lover, and prophet or poet,[4] they are different manifestations of the same quest. Here we find Yeats at his most didactic – the choices of all seekers are finally for spiritual transcendence, for raising themselves and their fellow men above the confines of mortality. Moreover, the seekers are often described with images of light and fire which serve to set them further apart from other mortals and to link them with the gods outside time, the more perfected inhabitants of the otherworld who are also described with these images.

The highest goal of the seekers in Yeats's drama is to free themselves from their incomplete and therefore unhappy state in the journey through the cycles of the universe. Just as important, however, and more feasible, is to achieve a spiritual cleansing, a spiritual regeneration in this life, not only for themselves but for all humankind and for the age itself. This is the goal that Yeats emphasized and, in his role as dramatist, strived for in the plays. Thus the issue of chance and choice brings out the dogmatic force of the philosophy in the drama. The theme of burning introduces this issue with a prophetic urgency that seeks to present enlightened people with viable choices for working with the coming spiritual influx, an influx Yeats strongly believed in, in

3 Yeats understood nothingness to be complete darkness, hidden by the "bewildering lights" of the nearly perfected spirits such as the Danaans (*DrC* 81). Nevertheless, just as he preferred to depict a golden paradise to an abyss in his drama, he also depicted the search for perfection, more often than not, as a search for the light. This was also the practice of the rituals of the Golden Dawn, in which aspirants are reminded that they are "indeed in a Path of Darkness groping for Light" (I. Regardie, *The Golden Dawn: An Account of the Teachings, Rites and Ceremonies of the Order of the Golden Dawn*, vol. 1 [4 vols; Chicago: Aries Press, 1937-40], p. 187, quoted in *DrC* 29).

4 In Yeats's story "The Tables of the Law," Owen Aherne states that he "shall send out of this chapel saints, lovers, rebels and prophets: souls that will surround themselves with peace, as with a nest made of grass" (*M* 302).

order to bring about spiritual regeneration for the individual and for the age.

Chance

The larger forces of chance clearly influence, even tamper with, the lives of many of the protagonists in Yeats's drama. On the most obvious level they are the God-figures in the plays, from the Christian God in *The Countess Cathleen*, whose intervention saves Cathleen from the clutches of the devils, and rewards her with a spectacular reception into heaven, accompanied by a great deal of fanfare and as many angels as the Abbey Theatre's limited stage could hold, to Manannan in *Deirdre*, *The Golden Helmet*, and other plays, to the Great Herne, the Unicorn, and all the other personifications of fate. They are also the forces of generation (creation) and destruction that these figures of fate have at their command. Within Yeats's system mortals are determined by less dramatic forces as well, particularly by the seemingly endless cycles around the lunar wheel that they must undergo before they can return to the beginning. During these cycles their circumstances and even their character are at least partly dictated by the external forces of the universe, and this they have little choice but to accept: "During its sleep in the womb the *Spirit* accepts its future life, declares it just" (*AV* (B) 235). These cycles are, for obvious reasons, difficult to depict dramatically, though they are referred to obliquely, as in the opening lyrics to *The Only Jealousy of Emer*; their closest counterpart in most plays are the cycles of succeeding ages that must perforce influence the individuals living within them.

Yeats believed not only that incarnate and discarnate spirits live each other's death, die each other's life, but also that the same thing applies to successive ages. (The correspondence between the cycles of an individual and of an age is similar to that between the individual memory and the collective or racial memory discussed in Chapter 3.) At the apex of one age, another is born which is its opposite in every sense, and which grows in strength as the first age begins to wane, and peaks as the first age dies. Yeats theorized that these succeeding ages are alternately objective, or *primary*, and subjective, or *antithetical*. These historical cycles to some extent determine the character and circumstances of the mortals living within them, and thus represent the forces of chance which impinge on the individual spirit. Nevertheless, they are themselves caught in the battle of free-will and determinism. In the words of Michael Robartes: "After an age of necessity, truth, goodness, mechanism, science, democracy, abstraction, peace

[*primary*], comes an age of freedom, fiction, evil, kindred, art, aristoc-
racy, particularity, war [*antithetical*]" (*AV* (B) 52).

Yeats wrote in "Per Amica Silentia Lunae" and again in *A Vision* that
each nation, like each spirit, has a daimon that molds it into its opposite
(*M* 362); clearly the same applies to succeeding ages, since the revelation which precedes the transformation of an age, and which is described in the notes to "The Second Coming," comes, like daimon to
mortal, in a lightning flash, oft repeated, until the age has molded itself
into its opposite (*VE* 823-24). The "scientific, fact-accumulating" *primary* age whose downfall Yeats predicted in these notes is the Christian
civilization in which he lived; a large number of the plays echo this
same prediction, and look to the *antithetical* age which must succeed it.
Nevertheless, though the *primary* age must inevitably embrace its
daimon and become its opposite, it has, like the spirit, a certain degree
of choice as to how quickly to heed the whisperings of its daimon. In
The Player Queen the prophet who will announce this new age will be
born of the union of the Unicorn with the Queen, but the Unicorn will
not beget, and so the coming age is continually postponed, to the
intense regret of the poet Septimus and, one assumes, of Yeats himself.

The coming *antithetical* revelation, whether announced by the offspring of the Unicorn or of the Great Herne, is thus just one in a long
series of revelations announcing succeeding ages which occur every
2,200 years. However, whether for dramatic effect or following the
tenets of his secret magical society, Yeats in a number of plays dove-
tailed the coming religious dispensation with one of the two great
catastrophes of the earth, the impending destruction of the world by
fire which follows the great Biblical Deluge, the destruction and restoration of the world by water. The clearest example of this is *The Player
Queen*, particularly as we now have at our disposal, thanks to Curtis
Bradford's diligent scholarship, over thirty manuscript versions of the
play, spanning the more than twenty years that Yeats spent trying to
rid his play of obsessive philosophic abstractions. Although the published versions of the play seem to announce only the coming spiritual
dispensation, in most of these early versions great emphasis is placed
on the story of the flood and of the coming destruction by fire, and only
by analogy on the coming spiritual changes.

Possibly in a last-ditch effort to make his play readily understandable
(though this would go against his normal practice) Yeats stated explicitly for the first time in the published 1922 version of the play that it
announces a new *antithetical* dispensation, though one that is slow in
coming. With lines that can have no other interpretation, Septimus
cries: "Gather about me, for I announce the end of the Christian Era,

Chance, Choice, and the Spiritual Seeker

the coming of a New Dispensation, that of the New Adam, that of the Unicorn; but alas, he is chaste, he hesitates, he hesitates" (*MPQ* 421). The last extant manuscript versions state this less explicitly, and place more emphasis on the frustration of Septimus at the reluctance of the Unicorn:

> I will die railing upon the unicorn because he will
> Not trample mankind to death under his hooves and beget
> Upon some woman a new race.
>
> (*MPQ* 406-407)

The Unicorn itself only makes an appearance in draft nineteen and, says Bradford, the "first apocalyptic hint in a play that was to become decidedly apocalyptic" (*MPQ* 145) only occurs in draft eleven. It is my contention, however, that the play is decidedly apocalyptic right from the beginning.

The early versions of the play focus on the growing dissatisfaction of the citizens with their Queen, who aspires to be a saint and not a ruler. Knowing Yeats's spiritual bent, it is evident fairly quickly that both the role of the Queen and her approaching demise have spiritual connotations, especially when an old man is introduced who is possessed by the ghost of the Queen's father and who announces the coming death of one monarch and the elevation to the throne of another by braying with the voice of the donkey who carried Jesus into Jerusalem. The old man's role is to announce the coming change in the world from the old order to the new. This change is being hurried on by the enraged citizens who, as their discontent mounts, band together to storm the castle and replace the Queen with a more able ruler.

This plot is juxtaposed against a sub-plot in which a group of players, at the Queen's request, are attempting to stage a play, called "The Tragical History of Noah's Deluge," within the besieged castle. F. A. C. Wilson first pointed to the real significance of this play, which he calls "an ingenious piece of symbolism in which Yeats remembers Blake":

No one who has read the Quaritch edition could fail to remember, as one of Yeats's most successful pieces of exegesis, those pages in which he relates Blake's image of Noah's Ark to his author's cyclic theory of history, and explains that "the destruction of all things by the flood" is a symbol for the disaster that overtakes humanity at the end of a cycle.[5]

Wilson's assessment of the importance of this theme has received little attention, perhaps because in the published versions of *The Player Queen* the Noah play has been reduced to a recurring, seemingly

5 F. A. C. Wilson, *W. B. Yeats and Tradition* (London: Methuen, 1968), p. 183.

unintegrated motif; it was chosen, we are told, for the simple reason that the religious Queen will only tolerate plays based on real and holy stories. However, we now know that Yeats spent much of his time in the early versions elaborating on the themes of this play-within-a-play. The Noah play is in fact portentous and timely, though this fact is lost on all the populace present at its performance (with the exception of the fool) and is even lost on the editor of these manuscripts, who does not understand why Yeats insisted on including it. Writes Bradford, "I cannot see that staging the Noah play advanced Yeats's purpose in any way and can only conclude that, since *Hamlet*, the play within the play has had a morbid fascination for playwrights" (*MPQ* 11). Elsewhere he concludes that "The Noah play is there to provide a dull part for Decima to dislike" (*MPQ* 255).

Mad Michael, the fool of drafts eleven and twelve, understands the significance of the destruction by water which the play is dramatizing, though his babbling is ignored by the audience. He states,

Before the flood men were spirits, nothing but spirits. But afterwards they had bodies. The flood of space and the flood of time they call it. Those that were drowned did not die. No, no. They were the people that became like the beasts, a multitude of things. They changed, they change, they change always. But those in the Ark now, they do not change, oh no.

(*MPQ* 137)

This speech helps explain the significance of the motif of drowning and of the parade of beasts that Yeats retained even in the published version. Michael is alluding to the mystical traditions which teach that generation occurred through water, and is thus equating the Deluge with creation, with, in Celtic terms, the streams that burst forth at creation from Connla's Well. The sudden thunderous force of creation, the rushing of everything out of nothing, is quite beautifully represented by the awesome force of the flood. Yeats elaborated this theory in *A Vision*, where he posited that the world is destroyed once by water and once by fire in the course of every Great Year.[6] The destruction by water is a creation of sorts, for it is by "a 'lunar' water that is Nature" (*AV* (B) 247) and is equated with Discord and separation (the fall from unity) while the destruction by fire is equated with Concord and unity (the joining of the many into the One at the end of time).[7]

6 Yeats's Great Year, somewhat different from Plato's, encompasses 26,000 years and therefore six *antithetical* and six *primary* ages (*AV* (B) 254).
7 The Deluge as creation is further elaborated in *A Vision*: "The destroying flood rose in Capricorn but lasted through the two succeeding signs, only disappearing when the World-Restorer appeared; the creation itself had been but a restoration. To many Christians and Jews, though the doctrine soon ceased to be orthodox, not the Messiah alone but the Spirit that moved upon the waters, and Noah on Mount Ararat, seemed such world-restorers" (*AV* (B) 249).

At creation spirits enter the universe of "time and fate and change," as Yeats called the world in a number of plays, donning bodies and becoming "wet" or incarnate souls, in contrast to the dry souls of discarnate spirits such as the Hawk Woman in *At the Hawk's Well*, of whom the Old Man says, "There falls a curse / On all who have gazed in her unmoistened eyes" (*VP1* 407). Spirits, Michael states, were thus drowned into material form, following Yeats's belief that spirits die into our life as we die into the spiritual life. This is the significance of the mask of Noah's sister with the "beautiful, drowned, flighty mouth" (*VP1* 753) which Decima puts on at the end of the final version of the play. Noah's sister, unlike his ugly wife, refused to follow Noah's command to enter the Ark and was thus drowned into material form (*VP1* 749). In the broader context of chance and choice, the Deluge is the first manifestation of God's choice (humanity's chance). The following versions of the play emphasize its next and perhaps most powerful manifestation, the impending destruction of the world by fire.

In draft sixteen it is Yellow Martin (Septimus) himself who explains the significance of the Noah play in his "Prologue," but now its significance is more clearly tied to the troubled present, and to the coming destruction of the world by fire. He declaims, "Nobles and gentlemen, now let your troubles cease. The world is safe awhile. It has yet to be consumed by fire – that is the consuming of all forms and images – but once it was near drowned by water. From water generation comes, but that's a mystery" (*MPQ* 221). Septimus implies that the destruction by fire will have a different effect. Water gives life ("water is the mother of change," he says in another version) and thus gives rise to form, while fire will destroy "all forms and images." But Septimus does not continue, for he is interrupted by the attack on the castle, and the actors scatter in the ensuing confusion. The world is obviously not quite as safe as Septimus fondly believes; "the times are desperate" (*MPQ* 208), says the Prime Minister in the same version, while in another, Peter, one of the actors, cries that the people are about to set the castle on fire: "I heard them say 'burn down the Queen's house, / Throw everything that belongs to her into the flames'" (*MPQ* 138).

That these times are as troubled as were the times before the flood is implied everywhere in the drama. The parallels to Yeats's own time are also abundant. Perhaps the most obvious are the allusions to the corrupt taste of the theatre-goers who, like the audiences in Yeats's own time, demand realistic drama instead of the romantic but unpopular plays that Septimus wrote in his youth and that Decima longs to act in. These plays sound suspiciously like Yeats's dance plays, the "antiquated romantic stuff" which the Old Man speaks of in the "Prologue" to *The Death of Cuchulain* (*VP1* 1051). Therefore, long before it is made explicit in the play that a new spiritual dispensation is at hand, long before the Unicorn is introduced or before Septimus announces "the end of the Christian Era," the parallels between these evil times and the evil times preceding the flood make it clear that the play is decidedly apocalyptic, and that it emphasizes the larger forces of chance which mold the destinies of human beings.

On the basis of this play, in which the prophecy of the coming cataclysm through fire is very plainly stated, it is possible to unearth traces of the same prophecy in a number of other plays. In *The Unicorn from the Stars*, Father John states explicitly that "the world was destroyed by water, it has yet to be consumed by fire" (*VP1* 674), though he is willing to wait far longer than is Martin for the destruction to take place. In *Where There is Nothing*, the play upon which *Unicorn* was based, Paul Ruttledge states that God's "last judgment" is approaching. Like the revelation of which Yeats speaks in the notes to "The Second Coming," this revelation or apocalypse will strike in different places over a period of time: "God will accomplish his last judgment, first in one man's mind and then in another. He is always planning last judgments. And yet it takes a long time" (*VP1* 1158).

Both Martin and Paul predict that it will come in a "frenzy" of laughter and destruction, while in *The King's Threshold* the dying poet Seanchan announces that a new race is being created in heaven in just such a frenzy, through a marriage which can only take place, interestingly enough, "in the wild middle of summer," that is the month of fire, July (Cancer):

> That marriage, because it is the height of life,
> Can only be accomplished to the full
> In the high days of the year. I lay awake:
> There had come a frenzy into the light of the stars,
> And they were coming nearer, and I knew
> All in a minute they were about to marry
> Clods out upon the ploughlands, to beget
> A mightier race than any that has been.
> ....
> Laughing, it would take the mastery of the world.[8]
> (*VP1* 301)

This same prophecy seems to occur, though heavily veiled, in *The Hour-Glass*, one of the few plays that on the surface at least does not

---

8 Note the resemblance to the dung-covered swineherd in *The Full Moon in March* whose severed head laughs with the Queen as she dances before it in a dance symbolizing their union (*VP1* 988-89).

allude to spiritual influxes. In words very similar to those used by
Seanchan, the Wise Man describes his harried state after he has had
recurring dreams of the "otherworld":

> Reason is growing dim;
> A moment more and Frenzy will beat his drum
> And laugh aloud and scream;
> And I must dance in the dream.
>
> (*VP1* 587)

Could this scream be "the scream of Juno's peacock" (*AV* (B) 268),
which announces the coming dispensation?

The prophecy of a coming cataclysm through fire is repeated too
insistently throughout Yeats's work to be ignored. Nevertheless, while
the physical destruction of the universe through a consuming fire is the
perfect symbol for depicting the power of the forces of chance, it may
not be necessary to take this symbol literally. The fire, we remember, is
"a fire that is not what we call fire but 'the fire of heaven,'" and Yeats
himself was not entirely certain whether the consequence of this fire
would be complete annihilation, or merely a transformation, of the
world. Thus he queried in *A Vision*, "Was the world completely destroyed at the solstice or did it but acquire a new shape?" (*AV* (B) 247).

Whether or not the world is physically destroyed is finally immaterial since, following Yeats's philosophy, the world is no more and no
less than a thought held jointly by God (the community of spirits) and
the individual spirit. In order to effect a transformation, then, what
must be destroyed is not so much the physical manifestation of the
world as its manifestation in the minds and hearts of human beings.
An obvious analogy is the science of alchemy. While the external
manifestation of the alchemical process is the transmutation of lead
into gold, this is, for the true alchemist, merely a symbol and a by-
product of the transformation of the human soul into spiritual gold.
Explaining the goal of the alchemists, the narrator of "Rosa Alchemica"
says that "they sought to fashion gold out of common metals merely as
a part of a universal transmutation of all things into some divine and
imperishable substance" (*M* 267). A famous alchemist, Basilius Valen-
tinus, continues the narrator, "compares the fire of the Last Day to the
fire of the alchemist, and the world to the alchemist's furnace, and
would have us know that all must be dissolved before the divine
substance, material gold or immaterial ecstasy, awake" (*M* 270).

Martin, Paul, and Seanchan all receive their knowledge of the impending destruction or transformation of the world through dreams
and visions in which they are given a taste of the otherworld. Many
protagonists in Yeats's drama experience similar dreams which make

them discontented with this world. It is in part because of such dreams that Decima in *The Player Queen* longs for death: "And yet yonder, it may be, beyond death, are all the things we thirst for: wild adventures among blue mountains, a lovely life we but see in brief dreams, and after we fantastically copy" (*MPQ*, draft sixteen, 236). It is during one of these dreams that Martin sees "a shining vessel" being dropped and trampled underfoot by unicorns, and hears a command to "Destroy, destroy, destruction is the life-giver" (*VP1* 669). Martin is awakened before the end of the vision and assumes that the Grail-like vessel represents the world that he must set out to destroy. Nevertheless, after he successfully burns down a sizeable portion of the town, Martin learns that he was wrong in assuming that it would do any good to destroy the material world, since what is material is finally of little importance, being but the mirror of the mind. In a later vision, he learns what Paul Ruttledge has known all along, that what should be set aflame is not the physical world but the immaterial self, the heart and soul.

Chance seems to have merged with choice. Is Martin acting as a free agent in choosing to foment a fiery revolution, or is he merely a pawn of the forces of chance, the means through which the world will be destroyed by fire? Certainly chance, in the form of "that other Will" which, Yeats says, "we meet always in the deeps of the mind" (*M* 337), has tampered with Martin's life, afflicting him with waking trances in which he is given a vivid taste of the otherworld and directives for joining it; when he awakes, Martin can no longer be satisfied with his humdrum existence in this life. In *Where There is Nothing*, Paul also claims to be led by the forces of destiny: "I am led by hands that are colder than ice and harder than diamonds. They will lead me where there will be hard thoughts of me in the hearts of all that love me, and there will be a fire in my heart that will make it as bare as the wilderness" (*VP1* 1141). Paul's words echo Yeats's description in "Per Amica" of the daimon, the "hand not ours in the events of life" who is both the beloved and the enemy. The daimon is, as we have seen, that Higher Self outside time, the self from which the individual was separated at creation. Because the individual spirit is but part of the whole, the daimon can be said to be the other part, and thus the external forces of chance weighing upon the spirit.

The influence of the daimon is felt by most of the protagonists in the plays. Cuchulain, in particular, states in play after play that he is guided by an unseen hand of fate. In *At the Hawk's Well* a "lucky wind" and a "charmed sail" have brought him to Scotland and to the well of immortality; he is certain that his fate will also lead him to the water of immortality, for

> Why should the luck
> Of Sualtim's son desert him now? For never
> Have I had long to wait for anything.
>
> *(VPl 405)*

Cuchulain is too cocky – his daimon is also his enemy, and will put every temptation in his path to ensure that the choice of immortality, when he finally makes it, "may be as final as possible": "The Daimon, by using his mediatorial shades, brings man again and again to the place of choice, heightening temptation that the choice may be as final as possible, imposing his own lucidity upon events, leading his victim to whatever among works not impossible is the most difficult" (*M* 361).

The full responsibility for the choice is Cuchulain's alone. In *At the Hawk's Well* he chooses to be seduced by the dancer instead of watching the well, and his life is cursed for his efforts; in *On Baile's Strand* he chooses to go against his instincts, to relinquish his wildness for the comfort of hearth and home, and is rewarded for his choice by having to murder his own son; in the final version of *The Only Jealousy of Emer*, a broken and middle-aged man, he chooses oblivion in Fand's arms and has to be rescued by Emer (through the intervention of *her* daimon, who has led her to make the most difficult choice possible, to renounce Cuchulain's love in order that he might live again). Paradoxically, it is only in *The Death of Cuchulain*, when Cuchulain truly chooses to give himself up to fate, stating like his son in *On Baile's Strand* that "whether I live or die is in the gods' hands" (*VPl* 504), that he can finally free himself from the vicissitudes of the human condition.

While they are led to make these choices by their daimon, the actual decision as to whether to follow or ignore their guidance is left to the mortals themselves. The proof is that in *The Unicorn from the Stars*, while Martin is not the only one to have visions from the otherworld – "You are not the first that dream has come to," Father John tells him – he is the only one who decides to act upon them. Both his father Andrew and Father John have been subjected to them in the past, but both are cowards, and have found means either of ignoring these dreams or of blending them into their normal lives, using them as passive outlets rather than as an inspiration to action. Much the same thing occurs in *Where There is Nothing*: although Paul initially persuades a number of monks to join him in the difficult path he has chosen as a result of his visions, they all prove to be cowards, and abandon him and the holy life one by one. And in *The King's Threshold* the poet Seanchan, who knows that the poet's visions are the purveyors of truth, is abandoned by his pupils when he chooses to die for his beliefs. Though choice can be dictated by chance, therefore, there does nevertheless appear to be a fine but real distinction between the two. In the words of the Prime Minister in draft sixteen of *The Player Queen*,

> And those that will not make deliberate choice
> Are nothing, or become some passion's voice
> Doing its will, believing what it chooses.
>
> (*MPQ* 208)

Choice

In the "Great Wheel" chapter of *A Vision* Yeats posited that, while chance and choice, now *Body of Fate* and *Will*, appear in a different balance in every individual, every mortal has some degree of freedom. Most Yeatsian protagonists choose to exercise this freedom, even in defiance of chance. A common choice is to defy the natural pattern of life and death by escaping from the mortal condition; this is attempted by Forgael, Oisin, Mary in *The Land of Heart's Desire*, and, of course, by Cuchulain. With the exception of Mary and, in some versions of the play, of Forgael,[9] these protagonists cannot shake the forces of chance so easily, as Oisin acknowledges quite explicitly at the end of *The Wanderings of Oisin*. Because he chose to flee with Niamh from the sorrows of the world, Oisin must return to suffer those sorrows more completely.

OISIN:

> O Patrick! For a hundred years
> The gentle Niamh was my wife;
> But now two things devour my life;
> The two things that most of all I hate:
> Fasting and Prayers.

SAINT PATRICK:

> Tell on.

OISIN:

> Yes, yes,
> For these were ancient Oisin's fate
> Loosed long ago from Heaven's gate,
> For his last days to lie in wait.
>
> (*VE* 24)

---

9 That Forgael is perfected enough to attain the object of his quest, at least in early versions, is implied by the "Three rows of hounds, the first dark, the second red, and the third white with red ears" which are painted on his sails and which, writes Bushrui, quoting from books on mysticism and from R. Ellmann, "'are clearly analogous to the three traditional stages of the Mystic Way; Purgation, Illumination, Union.' They symbolize the state to which Forgael has attained by renouncing the material world" (S. B. Bushrui, *Yeats's Verse Plays: The Revisions 1900-1910* [Oxford: Clarendon Press, 1965], p. 8).

The more that mortals choose love, the more they must experience what they hate; the more they choose freedom, the more they must experience its opposite: submission to their fate. This is reinforced by a passage in the 1925 edition of *A Vision*, where, referring to his plays *Deirdre* and *The Hour-Glass*, Yeats wrote that, "In the one case natural love is brought to the greatest height, and in the other intellectual search, and both [in the end] reduced to nothing that the soul may love what it hates, accepting at the same moment what must happen and its own being" (*AV* (A) 243). The 1903 version of *The Hour-Glass* opens to the boasts of the Wise Man that, "Before I came, men's minds were stuffed with folly about a Heaven where birds sang the hours, and about angels that came and stood upon men's thresholds. But I have locked the visions into Heaven and turned the key upon them" (*VP1* 596). By the end of the play his intellectual search has been turned on its head, and he is reduced to pleading with an angel and with the angel's emissary, the fool, for his salvation, and finally to accepting God's will at whatever cost:

> And knowing all I cry
> That whatso God has willed
> On the instant be fulfilled,
> Though that be my damnation.
> (*VP1* 637)

Yeats later discarded this version, feeling that, while the words were faithful to his philosophy, "An action on the stage ... is so much stronger than a word that when the Wise Man abused himself before the Fool I was always ashamed" (*VP1* 577). In the 1914 version fate imposes its will much more subtly upon the Wise Man. While in the first version he meets with an angel almost at the beginning of the play, in the final version the forces of destiny impose themselves first in dreams, tampering with both his dreams and those of one of his pupils in an effort to plant doubts about the validity of his world view. It is only when this fails that an angel appears and, after warning the Wise Man that he is about to die, threatens him with eternal damnation unless, in the hour of life that he has left, he can find one other person who still believes in the existence of God and the angels.

In these works, the protagonists must face what they have rejected, in order that the balance may be restored: Oisin, having escaped sorrow, must now fast and pine; the Wise Man, having denied, must now believe. Both characters undergo a reversal similar to that experienced by souls in Yeats's system in the state between lives which he calls the *Shiftings*, in which the good experience evil, the evil, good (*AV* (B) 231). The goal for all spirits must be not to attain any one state, but to experience all such states that their understanding be complete. The closer they come to abandoning any one pursuit and accepting what must be, the closer they come to freedom.

This theme is carried still further in *Calvary*, where Lazarus, Judas, and even Christ himself are forced to face the opposite of that which they desire. Lazarus, having longed for and then prized his death, is fated to be dragged back by Christ to the life he hated. Judas, who cannot stand the thought that Christ's will is more powerful than his own, chooses to defy Christ's choice to be the God of all humanity and, by so doing, thinks he has regained his freedom:

> I could not bear to think you had but to whistle
> And I must do; but after that I thought,
> "Whatever man betrays Him will be free";
> And life grew bearable again.
>
> (*VPl* 785)

By imposing his own choice upon God, Judas, in words reminiscent of Forgael's after he has wrested the secrets of life from the god Aengus and subjugated those lesser gods, the Fomor, claims that he has become at least God's equal:

> And now
> Is there a secret left I do not know
> Knowing that if a man betrays a God
> He is the stronger of the two?
>
> (*VPl* 785)

Judas may be right. By betraying Christ, he may have freed himself from the yoke of destiny. However, the play also presents the possibility that, like Congal in *The Herne's Egg*, who also thinks that he has foiled a god, Judas may in fact have been merely a pawn of God, duped into thinking that he is following his own will in betraying Christ. This is what Christ implies when he states that "my betraying was decreed that hour / When the foundations of the world were laid" (*VPl* 785); he continues, "if [the betrayal] / 'Twere the commandment of that God himself, / That God were still the stronger." But Christ himself has problems coming to terms with his own destiny. He longs to be the God of all people, and cannot accept that he is only one of many gods, that there are some people he cannot save. Though he claims to do his Father's Will (*VPl* 783), he has not really accepted his fate. Thus he says, rather impotently,

> My Father
> Even now, if I were but to whisper it,
> Would break the world in His miraculous fury
> To set me free.
>
> (*VPl* 784)

Because he has chosen to save all humankind, Christ must experience rejection by those he has come to save.

The inadequacy of the choices made by Lazarus, Judas, and Christ is apparent when they are juxtaposed against that of the dice-throwers at the end of the play. These are the Roman soldiers who gamble for Christ's cloak; they alone are content, and they alone are truly free, for they desire nothing, but simply accept what must be.

> FIRST ROMAN SOLIDER:
> Although but one of us can win the cloak
> That will not make us quarrel; what does it matter?
> One day one loses and the next day wins.
>
> SECOND ROMAN SOLDIER:
> Whatever happens is the best, we say,
> So that it's unexpected.
>
> THIRD ROMAN SOLDIER [to Christ]:
> Had you sent
> A crier through the world you had not found
> More comfortable companions for a death-bed
> Than three old gamblers that have asked for nothing.
> (*VP1* 786)

Since only the dice-throwers reconcile chance and choice, they alone escape the conflict altogether. In the notes to the play Yeats labels them objective or *primary* characters; in *A Vision* he proclaimed that some *primary* mortals, those nearing the end or the beginning of the lunar wheel, have a greater degree of freedom than is granted other mortals because their will is so perfectly reconciled to their fate. He wrote that in the phases between twenty-three and three (excluding one, which is a discarnate phase),

There is an approach to absolute surrender of the *Will*, first to God, then ... to Nature, and the surrender is the most complete form of the freedom of the *Body of Fate*. ... When Man identifies himself with his Fate, when he is able to say, "Thy Will is our freedom" or when he is perfectly natural, that is to say perfectly a portion of his surroundings, he is free even though all his actions can be foreseen.

(*AV* (A) 44-45)

Significantly, these phases are associated with fire, "with elemental fire because here all things are made simple" (*AV* (A) 24). In this context it is clear that the Wise Man in *The Hour-Glass*, who is also an objective character (*AV* (A) 243), demonstrates this complete surrender of the will to fate, that greater Will. After resisting for most of the play, the Wise Man at the end gives himself up to the forces of destiny, proclaiming their victory with words that echo Robartes's description of necessity in *A Vision*:

> And now that it's too late I see it all:
> We perish into God and sink away
> Into reality – the rest's a dream.
>
> (*VPl* 635)

That this reconciliation of chance and choice leads to perfection and, ultimately, to the escape from the cycles of time is evident even in the setting of *The Hour-Glass*. While the earliest set of the play was the Wise Man's study, a later design by Gordon Craig altered the set in significant ways, as Karen Dorn has pointed out.

In Craig's new design, the Wise Man's study is only part of the set. The desk, now in profile, is in an alcove at the right front corner, in shadow. From the study, a corridor of screens curves round to the left, disappearing back centre stage into light. This arrangement suggests that the Wise Man's place is at one point of a circular pathway, that his domain of learning is at the dark end of a path moving towards light. The set anticipates the circling, gyring, and lunar phases of Yeats's later imagery, the kind of movement Yeats already considered symbolic.[10]

The saint and the fool, because closest to the end of the lunar wheel, are the *primary* characters who have the greatest amount of freedom because, paradoxically, they exercise their will the least of all characters. In *A Vision* Yeats describes the saint of Phase 27:

His joy is to be nothing, to do nothing, to think nothing; but to permit the total life, expressed in its humanity, to flow in upon him and to express itself through his acts and thoughts. He is not identical with it, he is not absorbed in it, for if he were he would not know that he is nothing, that he no longer even possesses his own body, that he must renounce even his desire for his own salvation, and that this total life is in love with his nothingness.

(*AV* (B) 180-81)

This passage describes Paul Ruttledge of *Where There is Nothing* almost perfectly; by teaching others to shed all that which attaches them to this

10 Karen Dorn, "Dialogue into Movement," in Robert O'Driscoll and Lorna Reynolds, eds., *Yeats and the Theatre* (Toronto: Macmillan of Canada, 1975), p. 125. There are parallels between this set and the new set for *The Land of Heart's Desire*, the play in which the protagonist's choice to escape to the Faery Kingdom is treated as a true escape from the cycles of time. Says Dorn, "The original stage directions called for a kitchen room, with everyone except the Faery Child on stage the entire time. All argument about the two choices was in the dialogue. But in the new version, Yeats set the play in the kind of scenery he used for *Deirdre*: a room opening onto trees and beyond, using Craig's lighting, to a 'vague, mysterious world.' This new stage space gives greater coherence to the dialogue. Take, for instance, the love scene between Mary and Shawn which, like the chess scene in *Deirdre*, combines the words with the stage set. In the new scenery, the hearth and family are to the right, Mary's bench and book of poetry to the left, and beyond the mysterious wood with its silver light" ("Dialogue into Movement," pp. 118-19).

life and to *become* nothing, he is the closest of all of Yeats's protagonists to a saint-figure.

According to *A Vision*, those *antithetical* characters who approach the unity of being possible at Phase 17, which is a foretaste of the unity of being at the end of time, also achieve a balance of the two forces of chance and choice, and thus a greater freedom than do most people. Writes Yeats,

> He who attains Unity of Being is some man, who, while struggling with his fate and his destiny until every energy of his being has been roused, is content that he should so struggle with no final conquest. For him fate and freedom are not to be distinguished; he is no longer bitter, he may even love tragedy like those "who love the gods and withstand them"; such men are able to bring all that happens, as well as all that they desire, into an emotional and intellectual synthesis and so to possess not the Vision of Good only but that of Evil.
>
> (*AV* (A) 28-29)

For both these *primary* and *antithetical* characters, this greater freedom, which is less an exercising of their power of choice than a reconciliation with fate, or chance, is a form of blessedness, for they are becoming less fragmented, and thus nearing the point where they can withdraw completely from the conflict of opposites and be united with their daimon.

This point is best illustrated by the play *The Cat and the Moon*, in which the Blind Beggar (who represents the body, as Yeats explicitly states in the notes) and the Lame Beggar (who represents the soul), travel to the Holy Well of St. Colman to be cured. At the well they meet a saint who offers each of them in turn the choice between a cure to their physical ailment and blessedness. Says the disembodied saint to the Blind Man: "I am a saint and lonely. Will you become blessed and stay blind and we will be together always?" (*VPl* 798). The Blind Beggar chooses his eyesight, while the Lame Man chooses to stay lame and achieve blessedness. It is clear that the Lame Beggar has made the better of the two choices; the saint mounts his back in the symbol of their union and the beggar, though supposedly still lame, begins to dance.

All mortals can choose, like the Blind Beggar, to pursue material rather than spiritual goals. Like the historical and religious cycles which may postpone the inevitable and refuse for a time to become their opposite, the spirits may put off making that most difficult of choices for some time. Nevertheless, they will all come face to face with their daimon many times, in many guises, who will present them with the possibility of choosing blessedness, and they must in the end acquiesce. Chance and choice merge most easily in the seekers in the

drama, those who, like Martin Hearne and Paul Ruttledge, follow the
directives of their daimon even though their decision must lead to great
hardship in this life. Because they are for the most part exceptional
beings, the seekers are led to make the hardest choice of all – to relinquish their ties with the earth, to destroy the bonds of mortality and
light the fires of heaven in their hearts and minds. This is also the
choice prescribed for the Wayfarer, the initiate in Yeats's Celtic Mysteries. In the cauldron ritual the Teacher speaks as follows:

I break this staff ... I burn it in the fire ... for the little safe rules, the little
comfortable orders, that quieted the daring of the mind, the fear that kept the
feet from the rough places, are being put away for ever. I have given this staff to
the fire, that it may begin the work of burning the heavens and the earth that
there may be nothing but the soul of man.

(*CMK* 161)

One could easily mistake this speech for one of Paul Ruttledge's.
Following a number of visions, Paul Ruttledge understands that "We
must get rid of everything that is not measureless eternal life. We must
put out hope as I put out this candle [puts out a candle] and memory as
I put out this candle [as before] and thought, the master of Life, as I put
out this candle" (*VP1* 1039). Paul's choice is also the choice of the
magician and the alchemist, "the transmutation of the weary heart into
the weariless spirit" (*M* 269) which the narrator of "Rosa Alchemica"
understands rationally but, being a coward, cannot emulate. The
choices which Yeats is most interested in and which he highlights in
the drama are, like the alchemist's, clearly spiritual choices. Here Yeats
is at his most didactic – the choices of all seekers, whether rebels,
saints, lovers, or poets, are finally for spiritual transcendence, for
raising themselves, their fellow mortals, and their age above the confines of mortality and thus for bringing about the promised age of
spiritual regeneration, whether within or outside this world.

Seekers

The seekers in the drama, those who search out wisdom and truth at
whatever personal cost, are markedly different from the ordinary,
rational characters who are aware only of the physical world by which
they are surrounded, and ignore the more profound truth that can be
glimpsed in dreams or through the imagination. As Father John says in
The Unicorn from the Stars, "it is to those who are awake that nothing
happens, and it is they that know nothing" (*VP1* 650).[11] Like Martin

---

11 The irony, in the light of Yeats's beliefs, is quite evident; life is a dream from which the
enlightened strive to awaken; when fully awake they know reality to *be* nothing.

Hearne, who cries, "My soul is my own and my mind is my own. I will send them to where I like" (*VP1* 664), the seekers choose to dream and to follow the instincts and directives of their visions. These seekers can thus be seen as the forerunners of the new *antithetical* age, the coming "age of imagination, of emotion, of moods, of revelation" (*EI* 197).

According to *A Vision*, the precursors of an *antithetical* age live short but very full lives, like the ancient Greek heroes who burnt themselves out at an early age.[12] Writing after the tragic and early death of Robert Gregory, Yeats associated him with these men:

> Some burn damp faggots, others may consume
> The entire combustible world in one small room
> As though dried straw, and if we turn about
> The bare chimney is gone back out
> Because the work is finished in that flare.
> (*VE* 327)

The seekers in the drama are also associated with light and fire and, with the notable exception of Cuchulain, often go out in a blaze of light at an early age.

This is true of Martin Hearne, who is associated with gold and fire from the beginning of *The Unicorn from the Stars*; his trance has been induced by the reflection of the sun's rays on the golden coach he has been building. Mary in *The Land of Heart's Desire* is called by the Faery Child the "little bird with crest of gold" (*VP1* 209); her ambition is to escape with the faeries and "dance upon the mountains like a flame" (*VP1* 192). Cuchulain is also associated with light and fire: in *The Green Helmet*, for example, Emer refers to "His mind that is fire / His body that is sun" (*VP1* 446). Because these images of light and fire are also associated with the more perfected inhabitants of the "otherworld," they serve to link the seekers with spiritual enlightenment. Thus, when Martin is surrounded by a golden light at the end of *The Unicorn from the Stars*, the beggars cry, "There is a sort of brightness about him. . . . It is not to this world he belongs at all. He is over on the other side" (*VP1* 708). Even Cuchulain associates himself with the company of immortals who "love to blow a smoking coal / Till it's all flame" (*VP1* 522), rather than with the ordinary, cowardly mortals who surround him in such plays as *The Green Helmet* and *On Baile's Strand*.

The seekers in the drama, like Paul, Martin, and Cuchulain, live their lives, then, as Yeats predicted that all will in the coming age: "we

12 Speaking of the last *antithetical* revelation, Yeats speculated: "Was it because the older civilization like the Jewish thought a long life a proof of Heavenly favour that the Greek race thought those whom the Gods love must die young, hurling upon some age of crowded comedy their tragic sense?" (*AV* (B) 268-69).

will trust our own being and all it desires to invent; and when the external world is no more the standard of reality, we will learn again that the great passions are angels of God, and . . . to embody them 'uncurbed in their eternal glory,' even in their labour for the ending of man's peace and prosperity" (*EI* 197). The seekers are therefore seen as a threat, and rightly so, by those who prize comfort and material security above all else. Men like Father Hart and Maurteen in *The Land of Heart's Desire*, Thomas in *The Unicorn from the Stars*, and King Conchubar in *On Baile's Strand* can be said to represent the decaying forces of the *primary* age which are trying to suppress the emerging *antithetical* forces embodied in Yeats's golden seekers. Father Hart and Maurteen are the least harmful; vaguely sensing the threat implicit in Mary's dissatisfaction with this world, they try to lull her into forgetting her desire to escape. Thomas in *The Unicorn from the Stars*, on the other hand, sensing the threat first in his brother Andrew and then in Andrew's son Martin, sets them both to hard work and bullies Andrew until he has broken his spirit. At the beginning of the play, he has almost succeeded in doing the same to Martin, who is completely engrossed in the practical task of coach-making. King Conchubar, the representative of law and order in *On Baile's Strand*, is impelled by the same fear as is Thomas, and sets out to subjugate Cuchulain by making him swear to obey the hearth-fire.

The fire of the hearth, so contained that its vital force has gone from it, is a fitting symbol of the repressive forces of the world that seek to control Cuchulain and the others in the plays. The hearth-fire is given a prominent place in a number of plays, its primary function being to ward off the "evil" influences of the "otherworld" with which, in this case, the seekers are aligned. Thus in *The Only Jealousy of Emer*, Emer lights a roaring fire to protect Cuchulain from "the enchantments of the dreaming foam" that "Dread the hearth-fire" (*VP1* 939). She does not succeed, and in an odd twist on this theme, the god Bricriu forces Emer to renounce the hope that she and her husband will sit together by the hearth again (*VP1* 545) before he allows Cuchulain to return to life. Cuchulain is thus allowed to become a wild, untamed man once again. The hearth-fire is often used to try to confine the seekers to this world, and to restrain them from seeking too great a freedom. In the words of Father Hart,

> by love alone
> God binds us to Himself and to the hearth,
> That shuts us from the waste beyond His peace,
> From maddening freedom and bewildering light.
> (*VP1* 193)

When the idealistic protagonist Michael decides to join the army and fight for the cause of Ireland in *Cathleen Ni Houlihan*, his parents "Try to coax him over to the fire" (*VP1* 231); as Yeats writes in the notes to that play, the hearth represents the "things of this world" which it is sometimes better to sacrifice, particularly for such an ideal cause (*VP1* 234).

On Baile's Strand is the best example of what can happen when an individual agrees to be bound by the hearth-fire, by the institutions of the home, and of law and order. In this play Cuchulain is still, at the beginning, a wild, untamed man, "one of those that God has made reckless" (*The Golden Helmet*, *VP1* 451). He is portrayed as a man who has long shunned the comfort and security that this world has to offer, and instead "lives like a bird's flight from tree to tree" (*VP1* 493). As he explains in the early versions of the play, he much prefers the love of wild women, of

> The women none can kiss and thrive,
> For they are but whirling wind,
> Out of memory and mind
>
> (*VP1* 499)

– immortal women, in other words – to that of gentler mortal women who can be tamed and can, in turn, tame him. In this play he is surrounded by and contrasted to bosom companions like Daire who, though he once valued freedom as much as does Cuchulain, now declares that "that was folly / For now that I am old I know it is best / To live in comfort" (*VP1* 512); Daire and the others have exchanged freedom for the comfort and confinement provided by wives and children.

Conchubar and his followers decide that Cuchulain must be tamed at all costs:

> "How can we be at safety with this man
> That nobody can buy or bid or bind?
> . . . .
> He burns the earth as if he were a fire,
> And time can never touch him."
>
> (*VP1* 479-81)

Conchubar, arguing for the security of the state, commands Cuchulain to swear allegiance to hearth and home over a fire "That has been lighted from your hearth and mine" (*VP1* 493). Cuchulain at first refuses to do so, but finally, and with great reluctance, he agrees. At this, Conchubar instructs all the other kings to join him in the oath:

Now thrust the swords into the flame, and pray
That they may serve the threshold and the hearthstone
With faithful service.

(*VP1* 499)

Cuchulain soon learns that he has made a fatal mistake in choosing to obey King Conchubar instead of the dictates of his own heart, for that decision leads directly to the killing of his own son. The new generation, the new life-force, the new law, have been smothered by the forces of the old, decaying order. As the play closes, Cuchulain is seen rushing into the sea, sword upraised, half-crazed with sorrow, and convinced that every wave is Conchubar. It is therefore easy to sympathize when Martin Hearne in *The Unicorn from the Stars* makes the opposite decision, to free himself forcibly from the repressive forces of the old, decaying, and life-destructive institutions of church and law, those institutions represented by King Conchubar, with a cleansing fire that will make way for the new order.

In an essay which sheds a good deal of light on *The Unicorn from the Stars*, Warwick Gould points out that the theme of the physical destruction of the world by human beings paralleling that of the destruction of the world by God, is used rather extensively by Yeats not only in this play, but in many earlier works as well. Gould argues that Yeats derived it from the prophetic writings of Joachim de Flora, to which he was introduced by Lionel Johnson, and in which, it seems, this destruction connoted both the destruction of the old order to make way for the new order on this earth, and the destruction of the earth in God's last judgment.

Central to the concepts of Yeats's *fin de siecle* Joachitism is that of *Straminis Deflagratio*, the burning of the straw. It is the notion of the attempt to light the "fires of the Last Day," which later informs *Where There is Nothing* and *The Unicorn from the Stars*, that Yeats and Johnson took from genuine Joachimist sources.... *Straminis Deflagratio* is an oddly overlooked aspect of all Yeats's Troy imagery, and is the central notion in "In Memory of Eva Gore-Booth and Con Markiewicz":

Arise and bid me strike a match
And strike another till time catch.[13]

Flora believed that the reign of Christ was soon to be replaced by that of the Holy Spirit, and urged his followers to burn down the old institutions of law and the Christian church in order to make way for the new spiritual influx. Yeats himself acknowledged the debt of his apocalyptic vision to Joachim de Flora in the "Notes" to *The Resurrection*: "Our

13 Warwick Gould, "Lionel Johnson Comes First to Mind: Sources for Owen Aherne," in G. M. Harper, ed., *Yeats and the Occult* (Toronto: Macmillan of Canada, 1975), pp. 267-69.

civilization was about to reverse itself . . . ; because we had worshipped a single god it would worship many or receive from Joachim de Flora's Holy Spirit a multitudinous influx" (*VP1* 932).

Yeats was, at least for a time, quite seduced by the concept of *Straminis Deflagratio*. Such friends as MacGregor Mathers indeed aspired to a Martinist-inspired revolution similar to that undertaken by Martin Hearne. As Yeats wrote in his *Memoirs*, Mathers was "always expecting, as indeed all the visionaries of his time were, a universal war, and had made his wife learn ambulance work that they might join together some roving band" (*Memoirs* 106), just as Martin joins a group of beggars, and Paul Ruttledge a band of tinkers. The magician Maclagan, the Mathers figure in Yeats's semi-autobiographical novel *The Speckled Bird*, announces the imminent destruction and burning of the present order: "Things are going very quickly in the world in our times, and you and I may see the streets and factories burning. Then we who have seen the truth [?] will be listened to. We shall reshape the world" (*SB* 22). The dreamer Michael, the Yeats figure in the novel, is enchanted:

the fantastic lights and colours of the eastern skies suggested to his imagination armed figures gathering to overturn the present order of the world. . . . He half persuaded himself that the lights and colours and vapours suggested to him armed figures and not something else because his soul knew what was to come and would show him an omen.

(*SB* 53)

Martin in *Unicorn*, also a dreamer, greatly resembles Michael. Nevertheless, while Michael is like Septimus in *The Player Queen* (interestingly enough called Yellow Martin in early versions of that play) who bemoans the fact that the new age is so long in coming but does little to hurry it on, Martin decides to take matters into his own hands. When Father John pleads with him to have patience, saying, "the world was destroyed by water, it has yet to be consumed by fire" (*VP1* 674), Martin answers, "Why should we be patient? To live seventy years, and others to come after us and live seventy years, it may be; and so from age to age, and all the while the old splendour dying more and more" (*VP1* 674-75). Following what he thinks are instructions of a higher order given to him in vision, Martin decides to burn down the old structures of the world. "When we have brought back the clean earth and destroyed the Law and Church, all life will become like a flame of fire, like a burning eye. . . . We will go out against the world and break it and unmake it. . . . We will consume the world, we will burn it away — Father John said the world has yet to be consumed by fire. Bring me fire" (*VP1* 686).

Martin is thus abetting the forces of chance, as are the citizens in the early versions of *The Player Queen* who, increasingly dissatisfied with their ruler, replace the *primary* Queen with her opposite, the lowly-born, *antithetical* Decima. By choosing to aid the coming cataclysm Martin is in a sense becoming the Marxist idea of the historic hero, who incorporates the forces of change within him- or herself and becomes a catalyst for that change. This is what Yeats was hoping to transmit to his audience — the possibility of hurrying on the coming spiritual liberation from the decaying and life-destroying order of the *primary* Christian age by incorporating this change within themselves.

While Martin chooses physical violence, his goal is nevertheless a spiritual one: "We will destroy all that can perish! It is only the soul that can suffer no injury. The soul of man is of the imperishable substance of the stars" (*VP1* 691). Martin comes to realize that he was mistaken to attempt to burn down the physical world: in a later vision, he learns that what should be set aflame is not the physical world but the immaterial self, the heart and soul. Martin has taken over the role of the priest, that role dramatized in the earlier *Where There is Nothing*.

The philosophic base of *Where There is Nothing* is very similar to that of *The Unicorn from the Stars*, but it is far more obvious, which is why Yeats disliked this play and removed it from his collected works. The play is in fact one of Yeats's most abstract and most didactic, and the dour Paul is far less endearing than is the occasionally comic, occasionally tragic Martin. Paul is a saint-figure almost from the beginning of the play. At first, he is an unwilling witness to the stultifying effect of the modern, well-regulated existence of the gentry and, like Martin, has fantasies of destruction in which he dreams of pulling down his own house and even the world itself. He chooses instead to abandon his carefully ordered life and to join a wandering band of tinkers. Paul soon begins to preach, first to tinkers and later, when he joins a holy order, to the monks themselves. His sermons usually follow a trance in which he receives some revelation, and are so vivid that he soon has a devoted audience among the monks. It stands to reason that Paul, along with his small band of followers, is soon expelled from the order, since, being part of the old Christian church, it is threatened by new revelations of any kind. The monks seek shelter elsewhere, and the sermons continue.

Paul believes that "There is so much fire in the soul, in yours, in mine, in the soul of any old apple-woman in the market that if one could get it out it would consume the world" (*VP1* 1072). He teaches his fellow mortals to release this fire, by becoming completely still and meditating on a "dangerous thought" until a light forms in their heads.

This is the light which the Fool in *The Hour-Glass* refers to when he tells the Wise Man that he can see angels when he "gets quiet": "then something wakes up inside one, something happy and quiet like the stars – not like the seven that move [the wandering stars], but like the fixed stars [the condition of fire]" (*VP1* 590).[14] Forgael also experiences "a torch inside . . . [his] head / That makes all clear." It is this torch that makes him reject the material world, for ". . . when the torch is lit all that is impossible is certain, I plunge into the abyss" (*VP1* 323). The monks learn to light such a torch; one says that "When I was meditating, the inside of my head suddenly became all on fire" (*VP1* 1135), and another quotes Paul saying that "if a man can only keep his mind on the one high thought he gets out of time into eternity, and learns the truth for itself" (*VP1* 1127).

The high seriousness of all this makes the play almost comic, but in fact Yeats took these beliefs very seriously, and advocated a similar meditation, with a similar goal, in his essay "The Philosophy of Shelley's Poetry":

there is for every man some one scene, some one adventure, some one picture that is the image of his secret life, for wisdom first speaks in images and . . . this one image, if he would but brood over it his life long, would lead his soul, disentangled from unmeaning circumstance and the ebb and flow of the world, into that far household where the undying gods await all whose souls have become simple as flame, whose bodies have become quiet as an agate lamp.
(*EI* 95)

Paul is explicitly teaching a way of escaping the order of the cycles of time and rejoining eternity though, it may be, only for one "fiery moment." His own personal goal, like that of many of Yeats's seekers, is to escape the cycles permanently; thus he longs for death, which is, he says, "the last adventure, the first perfect joy, for at death the soul comes into possession of itself, and returns to the joy that made it" (*VP1* 1160). However, this theme is tied here, as elsewhere in the drama, with the theme of the spiritual renewal of man and of the age, even within the bounds of time, since implicit in the play is a condemnation of both the civic and religious orders of the day.

Paul is an idealized, almost humourless priest, and Yeats rejected this play partly because he could no longer believe in priests. The priests were the prophets of the *primary* age; now, at the end of such an

14 The soul can only attain its goal in passivity; Yeats would agree with Plotinus that, in Rist's words, "If we 'pursue' the One, of course we shall always tend to specify it, to see it under some particular aspect. We must learn instead to be passive, to let it come, as it will come if we take away our own restlessness, that very restlessness which prevents us from being like it" (J. M. Rist, *Plotinus: The Road to Reality* [Cambridge: Cambridge University Press, 1967], p. 225).

age, when religion had become empty at the core, the priests had passed on their mantle to the poets. Not surprisingly, the arts, and in particular poetry and poetic drama, are linked in much of Yeats's writing to *Straminis Deflagratio*, the fiery consummation of the world. In "The Tables of the Law," the narrator explains "the curious paradox... that the beautiful arts were sent into the world to overthrow nations, and finally life herself, by sowing everywhere unlimited desires, like torches thrown into a burning city" (*M* 294).[15] These unlimited desires are, as Michael explains in *The Speckled Bird*, sown by the images of heavenly beauty depicted by artists which make people dissatisfied with the imperfect beauty to be found in the fallen world, and make them long for the otherworld. The poet Seanchan in *The King's Threshold* goes further, calling poetry

> the scattering hand, the bursting pod,
> The victim's joy among the holy flame
> God's laughter at the shattering of the world.
> (*VPl* 267)

Nevertheless, Seanchan agrees that the arts can also be instrumental in the regeneration of this world. He argues that the world is an illusion held collectively by human beings as a result of looking at images created by poets from the beginning of the world:

> poets hung
> Images of the life that was in Eden
> About the child-bed of the world, that it,
> Looking upon those images, might bear
> Triumphant children.
> (*VPl* 264)

It follows that if poets are responsible for the present image of the world, they are even more responsible for transforming the world, by changing its image in the minds of mortals. This is understood in *The Player Queen* by the actress Decima, though not by the poet Septimus.

In several early versions of *The Player Queen*, Decima finds some plays written by a younger, more inspired Septimus which he has discarded because they are so unpopular, so different from the mood of the present day. She insists that if he would put on the plays, and allow her to act in them, they would transform the minds of the audience, and gradually the age itself. In a speech almost identical to one of Paul Ruttledge's, Decima urges Septimus in drafts eleven and twelve to

15 Warwick Gould claims that Yeats also learned this paradox from Joachim de Flora (Harper, ed., *Yeats and the Occult*, pp. 167-69).

Let me become all your dreams. I will make them walk about the world in solid bone and flesh. People looking at them will become all fire themselves. They will change, there will be a last judgment in their souls, a burning and dissolving. Perhaps the whole age may change, perhaps the whole age may learn.

(*MPQ* 132-33)

This is akin to Yeats's argument in his essay "Poetry and Tradition" that by contemplating beauty people can be set free, and "those who have been freed . . . have something terrible about them, a light that is unendurable to eyesight" (*EI* 252). It is for this reason, explains Decima in draft fifteen, that she wants to portray the beautiful, inspiring queens of his early plays instead of Noah's ugly wife: "I must be beautiful and have shining things to wear. I must grow greater and make all those that look at me grow greater. Bad or good, it does not matter. But I must be a fire, a light" (*MPQ* 170).

Septimus does not have the courage of her convictions. In the final versions, the now quite inebriated poet transfers all responsibility onto the Unicorn, and agonizes over its chastity because "His unborn children are but images; we merely play with images" (*MPQ* 421). He refuses to see that his own plays are just such unborn images; by staging them he would breathe life into these images and awaken similar ones in the minds of those who saw them. We are back to chance and choice. Septimus rails against chance for failing to conceive. He cannot, or will not, understand that he could himself bring about the coming changes. He is indeed a coward, a "yellow" Martin Hearne; instead of choosing, he drowns his will in drink.

Septimus and the Unicorn are quite closely identified in the later versions of *The Player Queen*. We are told that when the Unicorn "bathes by the light of the Great Bear, and to the sound of tabors, even the sweet river water makes him drunk; but it is cold, it is cold, alas! it is cold" (*VP1* 748-49). Septimus's drunkenness is due to a more prosaic drink, but he also bathes by the "light of the Great Bear"; he also is drenched with cold waters, and shivers "in the pale light of dawn" (*VP1* 718). The Unicorn thus becomes associated with mortality, with the condition of the drowned or drunken soul. In the 1922 versions it is equated with Decima as much as with Septimus; like her, it "will be terrible when it loves." Because Decima, unlike Septimus, chooses to act, by the end of that version Septimus is thrown aside and the Unicorn itself is forgotten; it is now Decima, the actress, who "seeks destruction somewhere and with some man she knows nothing of" (*VP1* 760). Decima dons the beautiful mask of Noah's drowned sister and attempts to usher in the new age herself, by becoming the perfect *antithetical* queen, the fiery embodiment of the new age.

The parallels between the idealistic plays of Septimus and Yeats's own are quite obvious. Unlike Septimus, Yeats persevered in writing "antiquated romantic" plays which he knew must be unpopular in such a rational age. He did so consciously, for he knew himself to be an *antithetical* man in a dying *primary* age, and thus a precursor of the new *antithetical* age which must soon take its place. While Yeats was attracted by such alternatives as *Straminis Deflagratio*, the physical destruction of the old order that would ensure its replacement by the new, he understood that such methods were neither particularly effective nor necessary. The coming dispensation could be brought on, and the age transformed, through an intellectual influx in the minds of human beings. He argued in the plays both by precept and by example that it is not necessary to wait impatiently for the Unicorn to beget; ordinary mortals can become prophets of the new age, and can bring it on themselves. This message is inherent in a number of plays, and is stated explicitly in *A Vision*: "*antithetical* revelation is an intellectual influx neither from beyond mankind nor born of a virgin, but begotten from our spirit and history" (*AV* (B) 262).

Choice seems to have merged with chance. In the context of the decaying *primary* order in which many of the plays are set, there is only one real choice for the golden seekers in the drama, no matter what their role. They must work with the forces of chance, to rebel against the life-destructive forces of this old order, and replace them with those of the new, life-giving *antithetical* order. Most of these seekers in fact embody within themselves, though it may be through their daimon, the coming changes. Though most of Yeats's plays support the belief that mortals are free to choose who and what they want to be, the choice is within a set, and therefore limiting, framework. The only real choice in the long run is spiritual awareness, since the only real goal, again in the long run, is spiritual perfection, the union with the daimon, that Higher Self, in the condition of fire. This is as true in Yeats's magical rituals as it is in his plays. Thus in "The Initiation of the Spirit," the last rite in the inner order of Yeats's Celtic Mysteries, the goal of the Wayfarer is described, in a speech which ties together many of the themes in this chapter, as "the Spiritual Life, the stilling of all choice, the end of the ways is the same, the incarnate is many, the discarnate is but one, all flames are in the flame" (*CMK* 237).

Human beings can choose when to make the decisions to which they are brought by their daimons, decisions that will lead, however slowly, up the spheres, but they cannot, ultimately, choose not to make them. Chance (as the external forces of the universe, or as the daimon, that other self outside time), and choice (as the individual spirit separated from these forces), are finally, like all opposites, like yin and yang, separate and yet inseparable, for together they form the complete circle, together they dance the cosmic dance.

> Considering that . . .
> The soul recovers radical innocence
> And learns at last that it is self-delighting,
> Self-appeasing, self-affrighting,
> And that its own sweet will is heaven's will.
>
> (*CP* 213-14)

5

The Completed Symbol

In his *Autobiographies*, Yeats referred to "personifying spirits" who "bring our souls to crisis," and who are indisputably the daimons of "Per Amica Silentia Lunae" and *A Vision*. He implied, however, that these spirits act from *within*: "I know now that revelation is from . . . that age-long memoried self, that . . . shapes the child in the womb . . . ; and that genius is a crisis that joins that buried self for certain moments to our trivial daily mind" (*A* 337). The daimon, according to *A Vision*, is the part of an individual which exists beyond the confines of time and space, that other self with which he or she will be united at the end of time (*AV* (A) 30); together they will form the "Ghostly Self" of the phaseless sphere (*AV* (B) 211). It now appears that the daimon may exist within the individual, in that "buried self" beyond his or her conscious life.

Yeats was already moving towards this understanding of the daimon in the 1925 edition of *A Vision* for, though he stated that the daimon is a being quite separate from the incarnate self and is, in fact, interchangeable with several others, he also stated that the daimon "carries on her conflict or friendship with man, not only through the events of life, but in the mind itself, for she is in possession of the entire dark of the mind" (*AV* (A) 28): "But there is another mind, or another part of our mind in this darkness, that is yet to its own perceptions in the light; and we in our turn are dark to that mind. These two minds . . . make up man and *Daimon*" (*AV* (A) 27). Yeats went much further towards identifying the daimon with the unconscious when he speculated in the last version of *A Vision* that "the whole system is the creation of my wife's Daimon and of mine" (*AV* (B) 22), rather than the work of independent spirits. The whole is an "expression that united the sleeping and the waking mind" (*AV* (B) 23).

Yeats made increasing reference in his later works to the unconscious of which the conscious life is but a fragment. In his essay "The

Mandukya Upanishad," he called the individual's unconscious self that "Self that never sleeps, that is never divided" (*The Upanishads* call it the conscious self) and opposed it to the conscious self, that "fragmentary, forgetting, remembering, waking" self (*EI* 480). Elsewhere he wrote that he "always sought to immerse [his mind] in the general mind where that mind is scarce separable from what we have begun to call 'the subconscious'" (*M* 342). Yeats would certainly have agreed with the view expressed in the ancient Hindu *Book of Consciousness and Light* that "at birth the two spheres of the psyche, consciousness and the unconscious, become separated. Consciousness is the element marking what is separated off, individualized, in a person, and the unconscious is the element that unites him with the cosmos."[1] Yeats may well not have known of this book, which was published for the first time in the West in the 1957 edition of *The Secret of the Golden Flower*. Nevertheless, it teaches meditations for uniting the unconscious with the conscious mind very similar to the method taught by Paul Ruttledge; for both, the ultimate goal is the freedom from division.

Since "revelation" (the dreams and visions induced by the daimon) comes from the unconscious, that "age-old memoried self," it stands to reason that chance, or the external forces of the universe, can also be understood to be a part of man, that part which he has forgotten at birth and must struggle to remember. Yeats implied this in *A Vision* when speaking of his plays *Deirdre* and *The Hour-Glass*. After stating that in those plays love and intellectual search are "reduced to nothing that the soul may love what it hates," so that, in other words, the soul which has chosen freedom may know its opposite, destiny, he proceeded to equate the two: the soul must accept "at the same moment what must happen and its own being, for the Ghostly Self [the permanent self] is that which is unique[2] in man and in his fate" (*AV* (A) 243). Chance and choice are thus, in the final analysis, merely warring forces within one being.

The division of the psyche into consciousness and the unconscious reflects the division of the One into the many at creation in the same way that "The whole passage from birth to birth" reflects "the whole passage of the universe through time and back into its timeless and spaceless condition" (Proposition V). Using the terms of Jungian psychology, which echoes many of the tenets of Yeats's philosophy,

1 Salome Wilhelm, "Introduction," in *Book of Consciousness and Light*, included in the 1957 edition of Richard Wilhelm, trans., *The Secret of the Golden Flower: A Chinese Book of Life* (New York: Harcourt, Brace, and World), p. xvi.

2 Yeats understood by the term unique "that which is one so cannot be analysed into anything else" (*AV* (A) 221).

the disintegration of the One can be understood on another level as the disintegration of the human personality, and all the spirits which struggle in the drama simply as warring, separate forces within one personality, and thus ultimately reconcilable.

There is considerable evidence for arguing that the action in many of Yeats's plays has both an objective and a subjective reality, taking place at the same time in Yeats's universe, a world in which matter and spirit meet, and in the microcosm of that universe, the individual mind. Yeats wrote of *The Hour-Glass* that "It is a parable of the conscious and the unconscious mind"; the same can be said of his other plays. A few examples should suffice, as attention has been drawn to this aspect of Yeats's drama by several critics, notably Helen Vendler[3] and B. R. Friedman.

In "Plays for an Irish Theatre" Yeats referred to this struggle within the minds of the protagonists in his drama: "It was only by watching my own plays that I came to understand that this reverie, this twilight between sleeping and waking, this bout of fencing, alike on stage and in the mind, between man and phantom . . . is the condition of tragic pleasure."[4] While Yeats consciously attempted to invoke this reverie in later plays through the use of masks which, "keeping always an appropriate distance from life, would seem images of the profound emotions that exist only in solitude and silence" (*VP1* 416), even his earliest plays reflect this concern. In *The Shadowy Waters*, Forgael undertakes a journey far out to sea which is, particularly in the early versions, quite explicitly a journey into his own psyche. Forgael's main problem is loneliness; his voyage is purportedly a flight away from the loneliness of self (*DrC* 196). Nevertheless, he is surrounded by gods who have been created by his own mind, "Fashioned / With his thoughts and desires" (*TPBS* xiii). These gods, write the editors of *A Tower of Polished Black Stones*, are the embodiment of his own emotions; "They are his perpetual rejection and destruction, in a fury of action, of all limited mortal experience" (*TPBS* xiv). His loneliness is thus compounded by the fact that, separated from himself (his Higher Self), he is nevertheless surrounded only by himself: "He is like a man living in a tower made of polished black stones which each reflect his face" (*TPBS* 44). The world and everything in it are merely his creations, his masks, and his costumes:

3 In "Changing Metaphors for the Otherworld," Helen Vendler argues that each of the groups of plays she analyzes dramatizes an encounter with the otherworld which takes place in the mind of the central protagonist (*Modern Drama* 7 [1964], p. 319).
4 Quoted in S. B. Bushrui, *Yeats's Verse Plays: The Revisions 1900-1910* (Oxford: Clarendon Press, 1965), p. 14.

```
For all                      &      souls    live
All souls that build the fire all things that He
                      and
Wraped up in fur or feather & bright with scales
                      that my
Are but malevolent masks for my own lips press
                      and
                      for
And cry through & the woods & waters and winds
Are robes but the robe I wrap about my head
And from of ald have shaken with my sighing
                                          (DrC 177)
```

    The confrontation between spirits and mortal characters in the plays, while very real in one sense, in another sense takes place in the subconscious, in "the deeps of the mind" of the protagonists. These spirits, from the human-headed birds in *The Shadowy Waters* to the Hawk Woman in *At the Hawk's Well* to Fand and Bricriu in *The Only Jealousy of Emer*, are both real communicators from the other world and personifications of those emotions which are raging within the protagonists – as if to underscore this point, Bricriu in the latter play actually dons Cuchulain's body.[5] B. R. Friedman argues very convincingly in his *Adventures in the Deeps of the Mind: The Cuchulain Cycle of W. B. Yeats*, that in most of Yeats's plays "the stage . . . [is] a mirror of the mind." Perhaps his best example is *The Land of Heart's Desire*, whose setting, writes Friedman, is a "psychic metaphor":

Ranged in the light around the hearth are the embodiments of the restrictions and responsibilities stifling Mary's spirit: Bridget, worn to bitterness by a life of housekeeping; Maurteen, valuing only the material comforts his labour has earned; Father Hart, demanding obedience to a repressive dogma; Shaun, offering a love doomed by mortality. Hidden by darkness beyond lies the fulfilment of Mary's dream wish, the Land of Heart's Desire itself.

Friedman continues, "The [Faery] Child's passage from the night outside to the light inside projects the emergence of Mary's wish into consciousness. Yeats's scenario captures dramatically the process Blake had defined as imagination: turning mental states into personified images."[6]

5 This practice of creating spiritual characters with both an objective and a subjective reality also has a precedent in Japanese Noh drama. Writes Richard Taylor of the play *Aoi No Ue*, which he claims influenced the writing of *The Only Jealousy of Emer*, "The Oriental model is a very simple ritual of spirit possession and exorcism in which a vengeful ghost is the personification of an emotion so intense that it has become an autonomous agent" (*The Drama of W. B. Yeats: Irish Myth and the Japanese Nō* [New Haven and London: Yale University Press, 1976], p. 140).

6 Barton R. Friedman, *Adventures in the Deeps of the Mind: The Cuchulain Cycle of W. B. Yeats* (Princeton, N.J.: Princeton University Press, 1977), pp. 18-19.

The goal for Yeats's seekers must be a reconciliation of these warring forces within themselves; it is for this reason that Paul Ruttledge urges his followers to still their thoughts until their mind becomes a single flame. The return to the One can thus be understood in alternative terms as a journey inward rather than upward. This is true as much for Plotinus as it is for Yeats. Writes Rist in *Plotinus: The Road to Reality*, "metaphors of ascent are not the only ones employed by Plotinus when he speaks of the soul's journey. He also frequently talks of returning or 'awakening' to our inner selves. . . . The soul *ascends* to the One, or *withdraws* from the external world to itself, or *returns* to its source or fatherland."[7]

The last step in the journey of the spirit in Yeats's metaphysics echoes the last step in the journey through consciousness described in the *Book of Consciousness and Light*, when the fragmented being is finally made whole. The end of this journey, like Yeats's nothing, or phaseless sphere, is symbolized in the text by a circle:

Without beginning, without end,
Without past, without future,
A halo of light surrounds the world of the law.
We forget one another, quiet and pure, altogether powerful and empty.
The emptiness is irradiated by the light of the heart and of the heaven.
The water of the sea is smooth and mirrors the moon in its surface.
The clouds disappear in the blue space; the mountains shine clear,
Consciousness reverts to contemplation; the moondisk rests alone.[8]

7 J. M. Rist, *Plotinus: The Road to Reality* (Cambridge: Cambridge University Press, 1967), pp. 215, 217.
8 *Book of Consciousness and Light*, in Wilhelm, trans., *The Secret of the Golden Flower*, pp. 77-78.

Selected Bibliography

Allt, P., and R. K. Alspach, eds. *The Variorum Edition of the Poems of W. B. Yeats*. London: Macmillan, 1957.

Alspach, R. K., ed. *The Variorum Edition of the Plays of W. B. Yeats*. London: Macmillan, 1966.

Bradford, Curtis B. *W. B. Yeats: The Writing of the Player Queen*. Manuscripts of W. B. Yeats transcribed, edited, and with a commentary by Curtis B. Bradford. Dekalb: Northern Illinois University Press, 1977.

Bridges, U., ed. *W. B. Yeats and T. Sturge Moore: Their Correspondence, 1901-1937*. New York: Oxford University Press, 1953.

Clark, David R., and George P. Mayhew, eds. *A Tower of Polished Black Stones: Early Version of "The Shadowy Waters."* Dublin: Dolmen Press, 1971.

Donoghue, Denis, transcriber and ed. *Memoirs of W. B. Yeats*. New York: Macmillan, 1973.

Frayne, John P., ed. *Uncollected Prose of W. B. Yeats*. Vol. 1. New York: Columbia University Press, 1970.

Frayne, John P., and Colton Johnson, eds. *Uncollected Prose of W. B. Yeats*. Vol. 2. London: Macmillan, 1975.

McHugh, Roger, ed. *Ah, Sweet Dancer*. New York: Macmillan, 1970.

O'Donnell, William H., ed. *The Speckled Bird with Variant Versions*. Toronto: McClelland & Stewart, 1976.

Sidnell, Michael J., George P. Mayhew, and David R. Clark. *Druid Craft: The Writing of "The Shadowy Waters."* Manuscripts of W. B. Yeats I. Edited by David R. Clark. Dublin: Dolmen Press, 1971.

Wade, Allan, ed. *The Letters of W. B. Yeats*. New York: Macmillan, 1955.

Wellesley, Dorothy. *Letters on Poetry from W. B. Yeats to Dorothy Wellesley*. London: Oxford University Press, 1940.

Yeats, William Butler. *A Vision*. London: T. Werner Laurie, 1925.

————. *A Vision*. London: Macmillan, 1937.

————. *Autobiographies*. London: Macmillan, 1955.

————. *Autobiography*. New York: Macmillan, 1953.

————, ed. *"Beltaine": The Organ of the Irish Literary Theatre* 1-3 (May 1889-April 1900).

————— . *The Celtic Twilight*. Dublin: Maunsel, 1905.

————— . *The Countess Cathleen and Various Legends and Lyrics*. London: T. Fisher Unwin, 1892.

————— . *Collected Poems of W. B. Yeats*. 2d ed. London: Macmillan, 1950.

————— . *Collected Plays of W. B. Yeats*. 2d ed. London: Macmillan, 1952.

————— . *The Cutting of an Agate*. London: Macmillan, 1912.

————— . *Discoveries*. Dublin: Dun Emer Press, 1907.

————— . *Essays*. 3d ed., rev. New York: Macmillan, 1924.

————— . *Essays and Introductions*. London: Macmillan, 1961.

————— . *Explorations*. London: Macmillan, 1962.

————— . *Four Plays for Dancers*. London: Macmillan, 1921.

————— , ed. *Fairy and Folk Tales of Ireland*. New York: Macmillan, 1973.

————— . *John Sherman and Dhoya*. Edited by Richard J. Finneran. Detroit: Wayne State University Press, 1969.

————— . *Mythologies*. London: Macmillan, 1959.

————— . *On the Boiler*. Dublin: Cuala Press, 1939.

————— . *Pages from a Diary Written in Nineteen Hundred and Thirty*. Dublin: Cuala Press, 1944.

————— . *Plays and Controversies*. London: Macmillan, 1923.

————— . *The Secret Rose*. London: Lawrence & Bullen, 1897.

————— , ed. and trans. with Shri Purohit Swami. *The Ten Principal Upanishads*. New York: Macmillan, 1937.

————— . *Two Plays for Dancers*. London: Cuala Press, 1919.

————— . *Wheels and Butterflies*. London: Macmillan, 1934.

————— . *Where There is Nothing*. London: Bullen, 1903.

Index